The History of Pyrrhus

Makers of History Series

Jacob Abbott

Cedar Lake Classics

Copyright © 2023 by Cedar Lake Classics

This is an annotated edition of a public domain work.

The History of Pyrrhus

CONTENTS

PREFACE vii
PHOTO INSERT ix

1. Olympias and Antipater 1
2. Cassander 16
3. Early Life of Pyrrhus 31
4. Wars in Macedon 44
5. War in Italy 58
6. Negotiations 72
7. The Sicilian Campaign 87
8. The Retreat from Italy 104
9. The Family of Lysimachus 116
10. The Reconquest of Macedon 131
11. Sparta 139
12. The Last Campaign of Pyrrhus 150

CONTENTS

ABOUT JACOB ABBOTT **171**
BIOGRAPHIES ABBOTT WROTE **173**

PREFACE

IN respect to the heroes of ancient history, who lived in times antecedent to the period when the regular records of authentic history commence, no reliance can be placed upon the actual verity of the accounts which have come down to us of their lives and actions. In those ancient days there was, in fact, no line of demarkation between romance and history, and the stories which were told of Cyrus, Darius, Xerxes, Romulus, Pyrrhus, and other personages as ancient as they, are all more or less fabulous and mythical. We learn this as well from the internal evidence furnished by the narratives themselves as from the researches of modern scholars, who have succeeded, in many cases, in disentangling the web, and separating the false from the true. It is none the less important, however, on this account, that these ancient tales, as they were originally told, and as they have come down to us through so many centuries, should be made known to readers of the present age. They have been circulated among mankind in their original form for twenty or thirty centuries, and they have mingled themselves inextricably with the literature, the eloquence, and the poetry of every civilized nation on the globe. Of course, to know what the story is, whether true or false, which the ancient narrators recorded, and which has been read and commented on by every succeeding generation to the present day, is an essential attainment for every well-informed man; a far more essential attainment, in fact, for the general reader, than to discover now, at this late period, what the actual facts were which gave origin to the fable.

In writing this series of histories, therefore, it has been the aim of the author not to *correct* the ancient story, but to repeat it as it stands, cautioning the reader, however, whenever occasion requires, not to suppose that the marvelous narratives are historically true.

* * *

Empire of Pyrrhus

Pyrrhus Viewing the Roman Encampment

1

Olympias and Antipater

B.C. 336-321

Situation of the country of Epirus.—Epirus and Macedon.—Their political connections.—Olympias.—Her visits to Epirus.—Philip.—Olympias as a wife.—She makes many difficulties.—Alexander takes part with his mother in her quarrel.—Olympias is suspected of having murdered her husband.—Alexander's treatment of his mother.—His kind and considerate behavior.—Antipater.—Character of Antipater.—Alexander's opinion of him.—Olympias makes a great deal of trouble.—Alexander sends Craterus home.—Alexander's wife Roxana.—Her babe.—Aridæus.—The two competing claimants to the crown.—Some account of the Ptolemaic dynasty.—The distribution of Alexander's empire.—Compromise between the rival claims.—Question of marriage.—Cleopatra.—Nicæa.—Nicæa is sent to Babylon.—Antipater's plan.—Another matrimonial question.—Cynane.—Excitement in the army.—Ada's new name.—Various intrigues.—Schemes of Antipater and Ptolemy.—Nicæa.—Perdiccas' plans.—A battle.—Craterus is killed.—Discontent.—Unpopularity of Perdiccas.—Transit of the Nile.—Extraordinary incident.—Great numbers swept into the river and destroyed.—The kings are to be sent back to Babylon.—Antipater returns to Macedon full of honors.

PYRRHUS, King of Epirus, entered at the very beginning of his life upon the extraordinary series of romantic adventures which so strikingly marked his career. He became an exile and a fugitive from his father's house when he was only two years old, having been suddenly borne away at that period by the attendants of the household, to avoid a most imminent personal danger that threatened him. The circumstances which gave occasion for this extraordinary ereption were as follows:

The country of Epirus, as will be seen by the accompanying map, was situated on the eastern shore of the Adriatic Sea, and on the southwestern confines of Macedonia. The kingdom of Epirus was thus very near to, and in some respects dependent upon, the kingdom of Macedon. In fact, the public affairs of the two countries, through the personal relations and connections which subsisted from time to time between the royal families that reigned over them respectively, were often intimately intermingled, so that there could scarcely be any important war, or even any great civil dissension in Macedon, which did not sooner or later draw the king or the people of Epirus to take part in the dispute, either on one side or on the other. And as it sometimes happened that in these questions of Macedonian politics the king and the people of Epirus took opposite sides, the affairs of the great kingdom were often the means of bringing into the smaller one an infinite degree of trouble and confusion.

The period of Pyrrhus's career was immediately subsequent to that of Alexander the Great, the birth of Pyrrhus having taken place about four years after the death of Alexander. At this time it happened that the relations which subsisted between the royal families of the two kingdoms were very intimate. This intimacy arose from an extremely important intermarriage which had taken place between the two families in the preceding generation—namely, the marriage of Philip of Macedon with Olympias, the daughter of a king of Epirus. Philip and Olympias were the father and mother of Alexander the Great. Of course, during the whole period of the great conqueror's history, the people of Epirus, as well as those of Macedon, felt a special interest in his career. They considered him as a descendant of their own royal line, as well as of that of Macedon, and so, very naturally, appropriated to themselves some portion of the glory which he acquired. Olympias, too, who sometimes, after her marriage with Philip, resided at Epirus, and sometimes at Macedon, maintained an intimate and close connection, both with her own and with Philip's family; and thus, through various results of her agency, as well as through the fame of Alexander's exploits, the governments of the two countries were continually commingled.

It must not, however, by any means be supposed that the relations which were established through the influence of Olympias, between the courts of Epirus and of Macedon, were always of a friendly character. They were, in fact, often the very reverse. Olympias was a woman of a very passionate and ungovernable temper, and of a very determined will; and as Philip was himself as impetuous and as resolute as she, the domestic life of this distinguished pair was a constant succession of storms. At the commencement of her married life, Olympias was, of course, generally successful in accomplishing her purposes. Among other measures, she induced Philip to establish her brother upon the throne of Epirus, in the place of another prince who was more directly in the line of succession. As, however, the true heir did not, on this account, relinquish his claims, two parties were formed in the country, adhering respectively to the two branches of the family that claimed the throne, and a division ensued, which, in the end, involved the kingdom of Epirus in protracted civil wars. While, therefore, Olympias continued to hold an influence over her husband's mind, she exercised it in such a way as to open sources of serious calamity and trouble for her own native land.

After a time, however, she lost this influence entirely. Her disputes with Philip ended at length in a bitter and implacable quarrel. Philip married another woman, named Cleopatra, partly, indeed, as a measure of political alliance, and partly as an act of hostility and hatred against Olympias, whom he accused of the most disgraceful crimes. Olympias went home to Epirus in a rage, and sought refuge in the court of her brother.

Alexander, her son, was left behind at Macedon at this separation between his father and mother. He was then about nineteen years of age. He took part with his mother in the contest. It is true, he remained for a time at the court of Philip after his mother's departure, but his mind was in a very irritable and sullen mood; and at length, on the occasion of a great public festival, an angry conversation between Alexander and Philip occurred, growing out of some allusions which were made to Olympias by some of the guests, in the course of which Alexander openly denounced and defied the king, and then abruptly left the court, and went off to Epirus to join his mother. Of course the attention of the people of Epirus was strongly attracted to this quarrel, and they took sides, some with Philip, and some with Olympias and Alexander.

Not very long after this, Philip was assassinated in the most mysterious and extraordinary manner. Olympias was generally accused of having been the instigator of this deed. There was no positive evidence of her guilt; nor, on the other hand, had there ever been in her character and conduct any such indications of the presence of even the ordinary sentiments of justice and humanity in her heart as could form a presumption of her innocence. In a word, she was such a woman that it was more easy and natural, as it seemed, for mankind to believe her guilty than innocent; and she has accordingly been very generally condemned, though on very slender evidence, as accessory to the crime.

Of course, the death of Philip, whether Olympias was the procurer of it or not, was of the greatest conceivable advantage to her in respect to its effect upon her position, and upon the promotion of her ambitious schemes. The way was at once opened again for her return to Macedon. Alexander, her son, succeeded immediately to the throne. He was very young, and would submit, as she supposed, very readily to the influence of his mother. This proved, in fact, in some sense to be true. Alexander, whatever may have been his faults in other respects, was a very dutiful son. He treated his mother, as long as he lived, with the utmost consideration and respect, while yet he would not in any sense subject himself to her authority and influence in his political career. He formed his own plans, and executed them in his own way; and if there was ever at any time any dispute or disagreement between him and Olympias in respect to his measures, she soon learned that he was not to be controlled in these things, and gave up the struggle. Nor was this a very extraordinary result; for we often see that a refractory woman, who can not by any process be made to submit to her husband, is easily and completely managed by a son.

Things went on thus tolerably smoothly while Alexander lived. It was *only* tolerably, however; for Olympias, though she always continued on friendly terms with Alexander himself, quarreled incessantly with the commanders and ministers of state whom he left with her at Macedon while he was absent on his Asiatic campaigns. These contentions caused no very serious difficulty so long as Alexander himself was alive to interpose, when occasion required, and settle the difficulties and disputes which originated in them before they became unmanageable. Alexander was always adroit enough to do this in a manner that was respectful and considerate toward his mother, and which yet preserved the actual administrative power of the kingdom in the hands to which he had intrusted it.

He thus amused his mother's mind, and soothed her irritable temper by marks of consideration and regard, and sustained her in a very dignified and lofty position in the royal household, while yet he confided to her very little substantial power.

The officer whom Alexander had left in chief command at Macedon, while absent on his Asiatic expedition, was Antipater. Antipater was a very venerable man, then nearly seventy years of age. He had been the principal minister of state in Macedonia for a long period of time, having served Philip in that capacity with great fidelity and success for many years before Alexander's accession. During the whole term of his public office, he had maintained a most exalted reputation for wisdom and virtue. Philip placed the most absolute and entire confidence in him, and often committed the most momentous affairs to his direction. And yet, notwithstanding the illustrious position which Antipater thus occupied, and the great influence and control which he exercised in the public affairs of Macedon, he was simple and unpretending in his manners, and kind and considerate to all around him, as if he were entirely devoid of all feelings of personal ambition, and were actuated only by an honest and sincere devotedness to the cause of those whom he served. Various anecdotes were related of him in the Macedonian court, which showed the estimation in which he was held. For example, Philip one day, at a time when placed in circumstances which required special caution and vigilance on his part, made his appearance at a late hour in the morning, and he apologized for it by saying to the officers, "I have slept rather late this morning, but then I knew that Antipater was awake." Alexander, too, felt the highest respect and veneration for Antipater's character. At one time some person expressed surprise that Antipater did not clothe himself in a purple robe—the badge of nobility and greatness—as the other great commanders and ministers of state were accustomed to do. "Those men," said Alexander, "wear purple on the outside, but Antipater is purple within."

The whole country, in a word, felt so much confidence in the wisdom, the justice, and the moderation of Antipater, that they submitted very readily to his sway during the absence of Alexander. Olympias, however, caused him continual trouble. In the exercise of his regency, he governed the country as he thought his duty to the people of the realm and to Alexander required, without yielding at all to the demands or expectations of Olympias. She, consequently, finding that he was unmanageable, did all in her power to embarrass him in his plans, and to thwart and circumvent him. She wrote letters continually to Alexander, complaining incessantly of his conduct, sometimes misrepresenting occurrences which had actually taken place, and sometimes making accusations wholly groundless and untrue. Antipater, in the same manner, in his letters to Alexander, complained of the interference of Olympias, and of the trouble and embarrassment which her conduct occasioned him. Alexander succeeded for a season in settling these difficulties more or less perfectly, from time to time, as they arose; but at last he concluded to make a change in the regency. Accordingly, on an occasion when a considerable body of new recruits from Macedon was to be marched into Asia, Alexander ordered Antipater to accompany them, and, at the same time, he sent home another general named Craterus, in charge of a body of troops from Asia, whose term of service had expired. His plan was to retain Antipater in his service in Asia, and to give to Craterus the government of Macedon, thinking it possible, perhaps, that Craterus might agree better with Olympias than Antipater had done.

Antipater was not to leave Macedon until Craterus should arrive there; and while Craterus was on his journey, Alexander suddenly died. This event changed the whole aspect of affairs throughout the empire, and led to a series of very important events, which followed each other in rapid succession, and which were the means of affecting the condition and the fortunes of Olympias in a very material manner. The state of the case was substantially thus. The story forms quite a complicated plot, which it will require close attention on the part of the reader clearly to comprehend.

The question which rose first to the mind of every one, as soon as Alexander's death became known, was that of the succession. There was, as it happened, no member of Alexander's own family who could be considered as clearly and unquestionably his heir. At the time of his death he had no child. He had a wife, however, whose name was Roxana, and a child was born to her a few months after Alexander's death. Roxana was the daughter of an Asiatic prince. Alexander had taken her prisoner, with some other ladies, at a fort on a rock, where her father had placed her for safety. Roxana was extremely beautiful, and Alexander, as soon as he saw her, determined to make her his wife. Among the thousands of captives that he made in his Asiatic campaign, Roxana, it was said, was the most lovely of all; and as it was only about four years after her marriage that Alexander died, she was still in the full bloom of youth and beauty when her son was born.

But besides this son, born thus a few months after Alexander's death, there was a brother of Alexander, or, rather, a half-brother, whose claims to the succession seemed to be more direct, for he was living at the time that Alexander died. The name of his brother was Aridæus. He was imbecile in intellect, and wholly insignificant as a political personage, except so far as he was by birth the next heir to Alexander in the Macedonian line. He was not the son of Olympias, but of another mother, and his imbecility was caused, it was said, by an attempt of Olympias to poison him in his youth. She was prompted to do this by her rage and jealousy against his mother, for whose sake Philip had abandoned her. The poison had ruined the poor child's intellect, though it had failed to destroy his life. Alexander, when he succeeded to the throne, adopted measures to protect Aridæus from any future attempt which his mother might make to destroy him, and for this, as well as perhaps for other reasons, took Aridæus with him on his Asiatic campaign. Aridæus and Roxana were both at Babylon when Alexander died.

Whatever might be thought of the comparative claims of Aridæus and of Roxana's babe in respect to the inheritance of the Macedonian crown, it was plain that neither of them was capable of exercising any actual power—Alexander's son being incapacitated by his youthfulness, and his brother by his imbecility. The real power fell immediately into the hands of Alexander's great generals and counselors of state. These generals, on consultation with each other, determined not to decide the question of succession in favor of either of the two heirs, but to invest the sovereignty of the empire jointly in them both. So they gave to Aridæus the name of Philip, and to Roxana's babe that of Alexander. They made these two princes jointly the nominal sovereigns, and then proceeded, in their name, to divide all the actual power among themselves.

In this division, Egypt, and the African countries adjoining it, were assigned to a very distinguished general of the name of Ptolemy, who became the founder of a long line of Egyptian sovereigns, known as the Ptolemaic dynasty—the line from which, some centuries later, the renowned Cleopatra sprang. Macedon and Greece, with the other European provinces, were allotted to Antipater and Craterus—Craterus himself being then on the way to Macedon with the invalid and disbanded troops whom Alexander had sent home. Craterus was in feeble health at this time, and was returning to Macedon partly on this account. In fact, he was not fully able to take the active command of the detachment committed to him, and Alexander had accordingly sent an officer with him, named Polysperchon, who was to assist him in the performance of his duties on the march. This Polysperchon, as will appear in the sequel, took a very important part in the events which occurred in Macedonia after he and Craterus had arrived there.

In addition to these great and important provinces—that of Egypt in Africa, and Macedon and Greece in Europe—there were various other smaller ones in Asia Minor and in Syria, which were assigned to different generals and ministers of state who had been attached to the service of Alexander, and who all now claimed their several portions in the general distribution of power which took place after his death. The distribution gave at first a tolerable degree of satisfaction. It was made in the *name* of Philip the king, though the personage who really controlled the arrangement was Perdiccas, the general who was nearest to the person of Alexander, and highest in rank at the time of the great conqueror's decease. In fact, as soon as Alexander died, Perdiccas assumed the command of the army, and the general direction of affairs. He intended, as was supposed, to make himself emperor in the place of Alexander. At first he had strongly urged that Roxana's child should be declared heir to the throne, to the exclusion of Aridæus. His secret motive in this was, that by governing as regent during the long minority of the infant, he might prepare the way for finally seizing the kingdom himself. The other generals of the army, however, would not consent to this; they were inclined to insist that Aridæus should be king. The army was divided on this question for some days, and the dispute ran very high. It seemed, in fact, for a time, that there was no hope that it could be accommodated. There was every indication that a civil war must ensue—to break out first under the very walls of Babylon. At length, however, as has already been stated, the question was compromised, and it was agreed that the crown of Alexander should become the joint inheritance of Aridæus and of the infant child, and that Perdiccas should exercise at Babylon the functions of regent. Of course, when the division of the empire was made, it was made in the name of Philip; for the child of Roxana, at the time of the division, was not yet born. But, though made in King Philip's name, it was really the work of Perdiccas. His plan, it was supposed, in the assignment of provinces to the various generals, was to remove them from Babylon, and give them employment in distant fields, where they would not interfere with him in the execution of his plans for making himself master of the supreme power.

After these arrangements had been made, and the affairs of the empire had been tolerably well settled for the time being by this distribution of power, and Perdiccas began to consider what ulterior measures he should adopt for the widening and extending of his power, a question arose which for a season greatly perplexed him: it was the question of his marriage. Two proposals were made to him—one by Olympias, and one by Antipater. Each of these personages had a daughter whom they were desirous that Perdiccas should make his wife. The daughter of Olympias was named Cleopatra—that of Antipater was Nicæa. Cleopatra was a young widow. She was residing at this time in Syria. She had been married to a king of Epirus named Alexander, but was now residing in Sardis, in Asia Minor. Some of the counselors of Perdiccas represented to him very strongly that a marriage with her would strengthen his position more than any other alliance that he could form, as she was the sister of Alexander the Great, and by his marriage with her he would secure to his side the influence of Olympias and of all of Alexander's family. Perdiccas so far acceded to these views that he sent a messenger to Sardis to visit Cleopatra in his name, and to make her a present. Olympias and Cleopatra accordingly considered the arrangement a settled affair.

In the mean time, however, Antipater, who seems to have been more in earnest in his plans, sent off his daughter Nicæa herself to Babylon, to be offered directly to Perdiccas there. She arrived at Babylon after the messenger of Perdiccas had gone to visit Cleopatra. The arrival of Nicæa brought up very distinctly to the mind of Perdiccas the advantages of an alliance with Antipater. Olympias, it is true, had a great name, but she possessed no real power. Antipater, on the other hand, held sway over a widely-extended region, which comprised some of the most wealthy and populous countries on the globe. He had a large army under his command, too, consisting of the bravest and best-disciplined troops in the world; and he himself, though advanced in age, was a very able and effective commander. In a word, Perdiccas was persuaded, by these and similar considerations, that the alliance of Antipater would be more serviceable to him than that of Olympias, and he accordingly married Nicæa. Olympias, who had always hated Antipater before, was now, when she found herself thus supplanted by him in her plans for allying herself with Perdiccas, aroused to the highest pitch of indignation and rage.

Besides the marriage of Perdiccas, another matrimonial question arose about this time, which led to a great deal of difficulty. There was a lady of the royal family of Macedon named Cynane—a daughter of Philip of Macedon, and half-sister of Alexander the Great—who had a daughter named Ada. Cynane conceived the design of marrying her daughter to King Philip, who was now, as well as Roxana and her babe, in the hands of Perdiccas as their guardian. Cynane set out from Macedon with her daughter, on the journey to Asia, in order to carry this arrangement into effect. This was considered as a very bold undertaking on the part of Cynane and her daughter; for Perdiccas would, of course, be implacably hostile to any plan for the marriage of Philip, and especially so to his marrying a princess of the royal family of Macedon. In fact, as soon as Perdiccas heard of the movement which Cynane was making, he was enraged at the audacity of it, and sent messengers to intercept Cynane and murder her on the way. This transaction, however, as soon as it was known, produced a great excitement throughout the whole of the Macedonian army. The army, in fact, felt so strong an attachment for every branch and every member of the family of Alexander, that they would not tolerate any violence or wrong against any one of them. Perdiccas was quite terrified at the storm which he had raised. He immediately countermanded the orders which he had given to the assassins; and, to atone for his error and allay the excitement, he received Ada, when she arrived at Babylon, with great apparent kindness, and finally consented to the plan of her being married to Philip. She was accordingly married to him, and the army was appeased. Ada received at this time the name of Eurydice, and she became subsequently, under that name, quite renowned in history.

During the time in which these several transactions were taking place, various intrigues and contentions were going on among the governors of the different provinces in Europe and Asia, which, as the results of them did not particularly affect the affairs of Epirus, we need not here particularly describe. During all this period, however, Perdiccas was extending and maturing his arrangements, and laying his plans for securing the whole empire to himself; while Antipater and Ptolemy, in Macedon and Egypt, were all the time holding secret communications with each other, and endeavoring to devise means by which they might thwart and circumvent him. The quarrel was an example of what very often occurs in such political systems as the Macedonian empire presented at this time—namely, a combining of the extremities against the centre. For some time the efforts of the hostile parties were confined to the maneuvers and counter-maneuvers which they devised against each other. Antipater was, in fact, restrained from open hostility against Perdiccas from a regard to his daughter Nicæa, who, as has been already mentioned, was Perdiccas' wife. At length, however, under the influence of the increasing hostility which prevailed between the two families, Perdiccas determined to divorce Nicæa, and marry Cleopatra after all. As soon as Antipater learned this, he resolved at once upon open war. The campaign commenced with a double operation. Perdiccas himself raised an army; and, taking Philip and Eurydice, and also Roxana and her babe in his train, he marched into Egypt to make war against Ptolemy. At the same time, Antipater and Craterus, at the head of a large Macedonian force, passed across the Hellespont into Asia Minor, on their way to attack Perdiccas in Babylon. Perdiccas sent a large detachment of troops, under the command of a distinguished general, to meet and encounter Antipater and Craterus in Asia Minor, while he was himself engaged in the Egyptian campaign.

The result of the contest was fatal to the cause of Perdiccas. Antipater advanced triumphantly through Asia Minor, though in one of the battles which took place there Craterus was slain. But while Craterus himself fell, his troops were victorious. Thus the fortunes of war in this quarter went against Perdiccas. The result of his own operations in Egypt was still more disastrous to him. As he approached the Egyptian frontier, he found his soldiers very averse to fighting against Ptolemy, a general whom they had always regarded with extreme respect and veneration, and who, as was well known, had governed his province in Egypt with the greatest wisdom, justice, and moderation. Perdiccas treated this disaffection in a very haughty and domineering manner. He called his soldiers rebels, and threatened to punish them as such. This aroused their indignation, and from secret murmurings they proceeded to loud and angry complaints. Perdiccas was not their king, they said, to lord it over them in that imperious manner. He was nothing but the tutor of their kings, and they would not submit to any insolence from him. Perdiccas was soon quite alarmed to observe the degree of dissatisfaction which he had awakened, and the violence of the form which it seemed to be assuming. He changed his tone, and attempted to soothe and conciliate the minds of his men. He at length succeeded so far as to restore some degree of order and discipline to the army, and in that condition the expedition entered Egypt.

Perdiccas crossed one of the branches of the Nile, and then led his army forward to attack Ptolemy in a strong fortress, where he had intrenched himself with his troops. The forces of Perdiccas, though much more numerous than those of Ptolemy, fought with very little spirit; while those of Ptolemy exerted themselves to the utmost, under the influence of the strong attachment which they felt for their commander. Perdiccas was beaten in the engagement; and he was so much weakened by the defeat, that he determined to retreat back across the river. When the army arrived at the bank of the stream, the troops began to pass over; but after about half the army had crossed, they found, to their surprise, that the water, which had been growing gradually deeper all the time, became impassable. The cause of this deepening of the stream was at first a great mystery, since the surface of the water, as was evident by marks along the shore, remained all the time at the same level. It was at length ascertained that the cause of this extraordinary phenomenon was, that the sands in the bottom of the river were trampled up by the feet of the men and horses in crossing, so that the current of the water could wash them away; and such was the immense number of footsteps made by the successive bodies of troops, that, by the time the transportation had been half accomplished, the water had become too deep to be forded. Perdiccas was thus, as it were, caught in a trap—half his army being on one side of the river, and himself, with the remainder, on the other.

He was seriously alarmed at the dangerous situation in which he thus found himself placed, and immediately resorted to a variety of expedients to remedy the unexpected difficulty. All his efforts were, however, vain. Finally, as it seemed imperiously necessary to effect a junction between the two divisions of his army, he ordered those who had gone over to make an attempt, at all hazards, to return. They did so; but in the attempt, vast numbers of men got beyond their depth, and were swept down by the current and drowned. Multitudes of the bodies, both of the dead and of the dying, were seized and devoured by the crocodiles which lined the shores of the river below. There were about two thousand men thus lost in the attempt to recross the stream.

In all military operations, the criterion of merit, in the opinion of an army, is success; and, of course, the discontent and disaffection which prevailed in the camp of Perdiccas broke out anew in consequence of these misfortunes. There was a general mutiny. The officers themselves took the lead in it, and one hundred of them went over in a body to Ptolemy's side, taking with them a considerable portion of the army; while those that were left remained with Perdiccas, not to defend, but to destroy him. A troop of horse gathered around his tent, guarding it on all sides, to prevent the escape of their victim, and then a certain number of the men rushed in and killed him in the midst of his terror and despair.

Ptolemy now advanced to the camp of Perdiccas, and was received there with acclamation. The whole army submitted themselves at once to his command. An arrangement was made for the return of the army to Babylon, with the kings and their train. Pithon, one of the generals of Perdiccas, took the command of the army, and the charge of the royal family, on the return. In the mean time, Antipater had passed into Asia, victorious over the forces that Perdiccas had sent against him. A new congress of generals was held, and a new distribution of power was made. By the new arrangement, Antipater was to retain his command in Macedon and Greece, and to have the custody of the kings. Accordingly, when every thing had thus been settled, Antipater set out on his return to Macedon, with Philip and Eurydice, and also Roxana and the infant Alexander, in his train. The venerable soldier—for he was now about eighty years of age—was received in Macedon, on his return, with universal honor and applause. There were several considerations, in fact, which conspired to exalt Antipater in the estimation of his countrymen on this occasion. He had performed a great military exploit in conducting the expedition into Asia, from which he was now triumphantly returning. He was bringing back to Macedon, too, the royal family of Alexander, the representatives of the ancient Macedonian line; and by being made the custodian of these princes, and regent of the empire in their name, he had been raised to the most exalted position which the whole world at that period could afford. The Macedonians received him, accordingly, on his return, with loud and universal acclamations.

2

Cassander

B.C. 320-316

Antipater's difficulties—Trouble with Olympias and Eurydice.—Character of Eurydice.—Her dictatorial and overbearing demeanor.—The convention of Triparadeisus.—Violence of Eurydice.—Antipater's life in danger.—Eurydice forced to submit.—Antipater is dangerously sick.—The arrangements made by him.—Antipater's arrangements for the succession.—Polysperchon.—Polysperchon invites Olympias to return to Macedon.—Cassander plans a rebellion.—His pretended hunting party.—Cassander explains his designs to his friends.—They agree to join him.—Olympias is afraid to return to Macedon.—War between Cassander and Polysperchon.—Curious incident.—Polysperchon's mine.—Success of it.—The conflict.—Consternation produced by the elephants.—Plan of defense against them.—The iron spikes.—Olympias finally concludes to go to Macedon.—Eurydice's troops desert her.—Olympias in her chariot.—Eurydice is captured.—She is sent to a dungeon.—Death of Philip.—Eurydice's despair.—he cell.—Eurydice's dreadful end.—Cassander's movements.—Olympias acts in the most energetic manner.—The siege of Pydna.—Movement of Cassander.—The carrying away of Pyrrhus.—Olympias resorts to a stratagem.—Olympias in prison.—Her end.

ALTHOUGH Antipater, on his return to Macedon, came back loaded with honors, and in the full and triumphant possession of power, his situation was still not without its difficulties. He had for enemies, in Macedon, two of the most violent and unmanageable women that ever lived—Olympias and Eurydice—who quarreled with him incessantly, and who hated each other even more than they hated him.

Olympias was at this time in Epirus. She remained there, because she did not choose to put herself under Antipater's power by residing in Macedon. She succeeded, however, by her maneuvers and intrigues, in giving Antipater a great deal of trouble. Her ancient animosity against him had been very much increased and aggravated by the failure of her plan for marrying her daughter Cleopatra to Perdiccas, through the advances which Antipater made in behalf of his daughter Nicæa; and though Nicæa and Perdiccas were now dead, yet the transaction was an offense which such a woman as Olympias never could forgive.

Eurydice was a still greater source of annoyance and embarrassment to Antipater than Olympias herself. She was a woman of very masculine turn of mind, and she had been brought up by her mother, Cynane, to martial exercises, such as those to which young men in those days were customarily trained. She could shoot arrows, and throw the javelin, and ride on horseback at the head of a troop of armed men. As soon as she was married to Philip she began at once to assume an air of authority, thinking, apparently, that she herself, being the wife of the king, was entitled to a much greater share of the regal authority than the generals, who, as she considered them, were merely his tutors and guardians, or, at most, only military agents, appointed to execute his will. During the memorable expedition into Egypt, Perdiccas had found it very difficult to exercise any control over her; and after the death of Perdiccas, she assumed a more lofty and imperious tone than ever. She quarreled incessantly with Pithon, the commander of the army, on the return from Egypt; and she made the most resolute and determined opposition to the appointment of Antipater as the custodian of the persons of the kings.

The place where the consultation was held, at which this appointment was made, was Triparadeisus, in Syria. This was the place where the expedition of Antipater, coming from Asia Minor, met the army of Egypt on its return. As soon as the junction of the two armies was effected, and the grand council was convened, Eurydice made the most violent opposition to the proceedings. Antipater reproved her for evincing such turbulence and insubordination of spirit. This made her more angry than ever; and when at length Antipater was appointed to the regency, she went out and made a formal harangue to the army, in which she denounced Antipater in the severest terms, and loaded him with criminations and reproaches, and endeavored to incite the soldiers to a revolt. Antipater endeavored to defend himself against these accusations by a calm reply; but the influence which Eurydice's tempestuous eloquence exerted on the minds of the soldiery was too much for him. A very serious riot ensued, which threatened to lead to the most disastrous results. For a time Antipater's life was in most imminent danger, and he was saved only by the interposition of some of the other generals, who hazarded their own lives to rescue him from the enraged soldiery.

The excitement of this scene gradually subsided, and, as the generals persisted in the arrangement which they had made, Eurydice found herself forced to submit to it. She had, in fact, no real power in her hands except that of making temporary mischief and disturbance; and, as is usually the case with characters like hers, when she found that those around her could not be driven from their ground by her fractiousness and obstinacy, she submitted herself to the necessity of the case, though in a moody and sullen manner. Such were the relations which Antipater and Eurydice bore to each other on the return of Antipater to Macedon.

The troubles, however, in his government, which Antipater might have reasonably expected to arise from his connection with Olympias and Eurydice, were destined to a very short continuance, so far as he personally was concerned; for, not long after his return to Macedon, he fell sick of a dangerous disease, under which it was soon evident that the vital principle, at the advanced age to which he had attained, must soon succumb. In fact, Antipater himself soon gave up all hopes of recovery, and began at once to make arrangements for the final surrender of his power.

It will be recollected that when Craterus came from Asia to Macedon, about the time of Alexander's death, he brought with him a general named Polysperchon, who, though nominally second in command, really had charge of the army on the march, Craterus himself being at the time an invalid. When, some time afterward, Antipater and Craterus set out on their expedition to Asia, in the war against Perdiccas, Polysperchon was left in charge of the kingdom of Macedon, to govern it as regent until Antipater should return. Antipater had a son named Cassander, who was a general in his army. Cassander naturally expected that, during the absence of his father, the kingdom would be committed to his charge. For some reason or other, however, Antipater had preferred Polysperchon, and had intrusted the government to him. Polysperchon had, of course, become acquainted with the duties of government, and had acquired an extensive knowledge of Macedonian affairs. He had governed well, too, and the people were accustomed to his sway. Antipater concluded, therefore, that it would be better to continue Polysperchon in power after his death, rather than to displace Polysperchon for the sake of advancing his son Cassander. He therefore made provision for giving to Cassander a very high command in the army, but he gave Polysperchon the kingdom. This act, though Cassander himself never forgave it, raised Antipater to a higher place than ever in the estimation of mankind. They said that he did what no monarch ever did before; in determining the great question of the succession, he made the aggrandizement of his own family give place to the welfare of the realm.

Antipater on his death-bed, among other councils which he gave to Polysperchon, warned him very earnestly against the danger of yielding to any woman whatever a share in the control of public affairs. Woman, he said, was, from her very nature, the creature of impulse, and was swayed in all her conduct by the emotions and passions of her heart. She possessed none of the calm, considerate, and self-controlling principles of wisdom and prudence, so essential for the proper administration of the affairs of states and nations. These cautions, as Antipater uttered them, were expressed in general terms, but they were understood to refer to Olympias and Eurydice, whom it had always been very difficult to control, and who, of course, when Antipater should be removed from the scene, might be expected to come forward with a spirit more obtrusive and unmanageable than ever.

These counsels, however, of the dying king seemed to have had very little effect upon Polysperchon; for one of the first measures of his government, after Antipater was dead, was to send to Epirus to invite Olympias to return to Macedon. This measure was decided upon in a grand council which Polysperchon convened to deliberate on the state of public affairs as soon as the government came into his hands. Polysperchon thought that he should greatly strengthen his administration by enlisting Olympias on his side. She was held in great veneration by all the people of Macedon; not on account of any personal qualities which she possessed to entitle her to such regard, but because she was the mother of Alexander. Polysperchon, therefore, considered it very important to secure her influence, and the prestige of her name in his favor. At the same time, while he thus sought to propitiate Olympias, he neglected Cassander and all the other members of Antipater's family. He considered them, doubtless, as rivals and antagonists, whom he was to keep down by every means in his power.

Cassander, who was a man of a very bold, determined, and ambitious spirit, remained quietly in Polysperchon's court for a little time, watching attentively all that was done, and revolving silently in his mind the question what course he himself should pursue. At length he formed a small party of his friends to go away on a hunting excursion. When he reached a safe distance from the court of Polysperchon, he called his friends around him, and informed them that he had resolved not to submit to the usurpation of Polysperchon, who, in assuming the throne of Macedon, had seized what rightfully belonged, he said, to him, Cassander, as his father's son and heir. He invited his friends to join him in the enterprise of deposing Polysperchon, and assuming the crown.

He urged this undertaking upon them with very specious arguments. It was the only course of safety for them, as well as for him, since they—that is, the friends to whom Cassander was making these proposals—had all been friends of Antipater; and Olympias, whom Polysperchon was about to take into his counsels, hated the very name of Antipater, and would evince, undoubtedly, the most unrelenting hostility to all whom she should consider as having been his friends. He was confident, he said, that the Asiatic princes and generals would espouse his cause. They had been warmly attached to Antipater, and would not willingly see his son and rightful successor deprived of his legitimate rights. Besides, Philip and Eurydice would join him. They had every thing to fear from Olympias, and would, of course, oppose the power of Polysperchon, now that he had determined to ally himself to her.

The friends of Cassander very readily agreed to his proposal, and the result proved the truth of his predictions. The Asiatic princes furnished Cassander with very efficient aid in his attempt to depose his rival. Olympias adhered to Polysperchon, while Eurydice favored Cassander's cause. A terrible conflict ensued. It was waged for some time in Greece, and in other countries more or less remote from Macedon, the advantage in the combats being sometimes on one side and sometimes on the other. It is not necessary to detail here the events which occurred in the contest so long as the theatre of war was beyond the frontiers of Macedon, for the parties with whom we are now particularly dealing were not directly affected by the conflict until it came nearer home.

It ought here to be stated that Olympias did not at first accept the invitation to return to Macedon which Polysperchon sent to her. She hesitated. She consulted with her friends, and they were not decided in respect to the course which it would be best for her to pursue. She had made a great many enemies in Macedon during her former residence there, and she knew well that she would have a great deal to fear from their hostility in case she should return, and thus put herself again, as it were, into their power. Then, besides, it was quite uncertain what course affairs in Macedon would finally take. Antipater had bequeathed the kingdom to Polysperchon, it was true; but there might be great doubt whether the people would acquiesce in this decision, and allow the supreme power to remain quietly in Polysperchon's hands. She concluded, therefore, to remain a short time where she was, till she could see how the case would finally turn. She accordingly continued to reside in Epirus, keeping up, however, a continual correspondence with Polysperchon in respect to the measures of his government, and watching the progress of the war between him and Cassander in Greece, when that war broke out, with the utmost solicitude and anxiety.

Cassander proved to be too strong for Polysperchon in Greece. He had obtained large bodies of troops from his Asiatic allies, and he maneuvered and managed these forces with so much bravery and skill, that Polysperchon could not dislodge him from the country. A somewhat curious incident occurred on one occasion during the campaign, which illustrates the modes of warfare practiced in those days. It seems that one of the cities of Peloponnesus, named Megalopolis, was on the side of Cassander, and when Polysperchon sent them a summons to surrender to him and acknowledge his authority, they withdrew all their property and the whole of their population within the walls, and bid him defiance. Polysperchon then advanced and laid siege to the city.

After fully investing the city and commencing operations on various sides, to occupy the attention of the garrison, he employed a corps of sappers and miners in secretly undermining a portion of the wall. The mode of procedure, in operations like this, was to dig a subterranean passage leading to the foundations of the wall, and then, as fast as these foundations were removed, to substitute props to support the superincumbent mass until all was ready for the springing of the mine. When the excavations were completed, the props were suddenly pulled away, and the wall would cave in, to the great astonishment of the besieged, who, if the operation had been skillfully performed, knew nothing of the danger until the final consummation of it opened suddenly before their eyes a great breach in their defenses. Polysperchon's mine was so successful, that three towers fell into it, with all the wall connecting them. These towers came down with a terrific crash, the materials of which they had been composed lying, after the fall, half buried in the ground, a mass of ruins.

The garrison of the city immediately repaired in great numbers to the spot, to prevent the ingress of the enemy; while, on the other hand, a strong detachment of troops rushed forward from the camp of Polysperchon to force their way through the breach into the city. A very desperate conflict ensued, and while the men of the city were thus engaged in keeping back the invaders, the women and children were employed in throwing up a line of intrenchments further within, to cover the opening which had been made in the wall. The people of the city gained the victory in the combat. The storming party were driven back, and the besieged were beginning to congratulate themselves on their escape from the danger which had threatened them, when they were suddenly terrified beyond measure by the tidings that the besiegers were arranging a train of elephants to bring in through the breach. Elephants were often used for war in those days in Asiatic countries, but they had seldom appeared in Greece. Polysperchon, however, had a number of them in the train of his army, and the soldiers of Megalopolis were overwhelmed with consternation at the prospect of being trampled under foot by these huge beasts, wholly ignorant as they were of the means of contending against them.

It happened, however, that there was in the city of Megalopolis at this time a soldier named Damides, who had served in former years under Alexander the Great, in Asia. He went to the officers who had command within the city and offered his aid. "Fear nothing," said he, "but go on with your preparations of defense, and leave the elephants to me. I will answer for them, if you will do as I say." The officers agreed to follow his instructions. He immediately caused a great number of sharp iron spikes to be made. These spikes he set firmly in the ends of short stakes of wood, and then planted the stakes in the ground all about the intrenchments and in the breach, in such a manner that the spikes themselves, points upward, protruded from the ground. The spikes were then concealed from view by covering the ground with straw and other similar rubbish.

The consequence of this arrangement was, that when the elephants advanced to enter the breach, they trod upon these spikes, and the whole column of them was soon disabled and thrown into confusion. Some of the elephants were wounded so severely that they fell where they stood, and were unable to rise. Others, maddened with the pain which they endured, turned back and trampled their own keepers under foot in their attempts to escape from the scene. The breach, in short, soon became so choked up with the bodies of beasts and men, that the assailants were compelled to give up the contest and withdraw. A short time afterward, Polysperchon raised the siege and abandoned the city altogether.

In fact, the party of Cassander was in the end triumphant in Greece, and Polysperchon determined to return to Macedon.

In the mean time, Olympias had determined to come to Macedon, and aid Polysperchon in his contest with Cassander. She accordingly left Epirus, and with a small body of troops, with which her brother Alexander, who was then King of Epirus, furnished her, went on and joined Polysperchon on his return. Eurydice was alarmed at this; for, since she considered Olympias as her great political rival and enemy, she knew very well that there could be no safety for her or her husband if Olympias should obtain the ascendency in the court of Polysperchon. She accordingly began to call upon those around her, in the city where she was then residing, to arm themselves for her defense. They did so, and a considerable force was thus collected. Eurydice placed herself at the head of it. She sent messengers off to Cassander, urging him to come immediately and join her. She also sent an embassage to Polysperchon, commanding him, in the name of Philip the king, to deliver up his army to Cassander. Of course this was only a form, as she could not have expected that such a command would have been obeyed; and, accordingly, after having sent off these orders, she placed herself at the head of the troops that she had raised, and marched out to meet Polysperchon on his return, intending, if he would not submit, to give him battle.

Her designs, however, were all frustrated in the end in a very unexpected manner. For when the two armies approached each other, the soldiers who were on Eurydice's side, instead of fighting in her cause as she expected, failed her entirely at the time of trial. For when they saw Olympias, whom they had long been accustomed almost to adore as the wife of old King Philip, and the mother of Alexander, and who was now advancing to meet them on her return to Macedon, splendidly attended, and riding in her chariot, at the head of Polysperchon's army, with the air and majesty of a queen, they were so overpowered with the excitement of the spectacle, that they abandoned Eurydice in a body, and went over, by common consent, to Polysperchon's side.

Of course Eurydice herself and her husband Philip, who was with her at this time, fell into Polysperchon's hands as prisoners. Olympias was almost beside herself with exultation and joy at having her hated rival thus put into her power. She imprisoned Eurydice and her husband in a dungeon, so small that there was scarcely room for them to turn themselves in it; and while they were thus confined, the only attention which the wretched prisoners received was to be fed, from time to time, with coarse provisions, thrust in to them through a hole in the wall. Having thus made Eurydice secure, Olympias proceeded to wreak her vengeance on all the members of the family of Antipater whom she could get within her power. Cassander, it is true, was beyond her reach for the present; he was gradually advancing through Thessaly into Macedonia, at the head of a powerful and victorious army. There was another son of Antipater, however, named Nicanor, who was then in Macedon. Him she seized and put to death, together with about a hundred of his relatives and friends. In fact, so violent and insane was her rage against the house of Antipater, that she opened a tomb where the body of another of his sons had been interred, and caused the remains to be brought out and thrown into the street. The people around her began to remonstrate against such atrocities; but these remonstrances, instead of moderating her rage, only excited it still more. She sent to the dungeon where her prisoners, Philip and Eurydice, were confined, and caused Philip to be stabbed to death with daggers; and then, when this horrid scene was scarcely over, an executioner came in to Eurydice with a dagger, a rope, and a cup of poison, saying that Olympias sent them to her, that she might choose herself by what she would die. Eurydice, on receiving this message, replied, saying, "I pray Heaven that Olympias herself may one day have the like alternative presented to her." She then proceeded to tear the linen dress which she wore into bandages, and to bind up with these bandages the wounds in the dead body of her husband. This dreadful though useless duty being performed, she then, rejecting all three of the means of self-destruction which Olympias had offered her, strangled herself by tying tight about her neck a band which she obtained from her own attire.

Of course, the tidings of these proceedings were not long in reaching Cassander. He was at this time in Greece, advancing, however, slowly to the northward, toward Macedon. In coming from Greece into Thessaly, his route lay through the celebrated Pass of Thermopylæ. He found this pass guarded by a large body of troops, which had been posted there to oppose his passage. He immediately got together all the ships, boats, galleys, and vessels of every kind which he could procure, and, embarking his army on board of them, he sailed past the defile, and landed in Thessaly. Thence he marched into Macedon.

While Cassander had thus been slowly approaching, Polysperchon and Olympias had been very vigorously employed in making preparations to receive him. Olympias, with Roxana and the young Alexander, who was now about five years old, in her train, traveled to and fro among the cities of Macedonia, summoning the people to arms, enlisting all who would enter her service, and collecting money and military stores. She also sent to Epirus, to Æacides the king, the father of

THE HISTORY OF PYRRHUS

Pyrrhus, imploring him to come to her aid with all the force he could bring. Polysperchon, too, though separate from Olympias, made every effort to strengthen himself against his coming enemy. Things were in this state when Cassander entered Macedon.

Eurydice in Prison

Cassander immediately divided his troops into two distinct bodies, and sending one, under the command of an able general, to attack Polysperchon, he himself went in pursuit of Olympias. Olympias retreated before him, until at length she reached the city of Pydna, a city situated in the southeastern part of Macedon, on the shore of the Ægean Sea. She knew that the force under her command was not sufficient to enable her to offer her enemy battle, and she accordingly went into the city, and fortified herself there. Cassander advanced immediately to the place, and, finding the city too strongly fortified to be carried by assault, he surrounded it with his army, and invested it closely both by land and sea.

The city was not well provided for a siege, and the people within very soon began to suffer for want of provisions. Olympias, however, urged them to hold out, representing to them that she had sent to Epirus for assistance, and that Æacides, the king, was already on his way, with a large force, to succor her. This was very true; but, unfortunately for Olympias, Cassander was aware of this fact as well as she, and, instead of waiting for the troops of Æacides to come and attack him, he had sent a large armed force to the confines between Epirus and Macedon, to intercept these expected allies in the passes of the mountains. This movement was successful. The army of Æacides found, when they reached the frontier, that the passages leading into Macedonia were all blocked up by the troops of the enemy. They made some ineffectual attempts to break through; and then the leading officers of the army, who had never been really willing to embark in the war, revolted against Æacides, and returned home. And as, in the case of deeds of violence and revolution, it is always safest to go through and finish the work when it is once begun, they deposed Æacides entirely, and raised the other branch of the royal family to the throne in his stead. It was on this occasion that the infant Pyrrhus was seized and carried away by his friends, to save his life, as mentioned in the opening paragraphs of this history. The particulars of this revolution, and of the flight of Pyrrhus, will be given more fully in the next chapter. It is sufficient here to say, that the attempt of Æacides to come to the rescue of Olympias in her peril wholly failed, and there was nothing now left but the wall of the city to defend her from her terrible foe.

In the mean time, the distress in the city for want of food had become horrible. Olympias herself, with Roxana and the boy, and the other ladies of the court, lived on the flesh of horses. The soldiers devoured the bodies of their comrades as they were slain upon the wall. They fed the elephants, it was said, on saw-dust. The soldiers and the people of the city, who found this state of things intolerable, deserted continually to Cassander, letting themselves down by stealth in the night from the wall. Still Olympias would not surrender; there was one more hope remaining for her. She contrived to dispatch a messenger to Polysperchon with a letter, asking him to send a galley round into the harbor at a certain time in the night, in order that she might get on board of it, and thus escape. Cassander intercepted this messenger. After reading the letter, he returned it to the messenger again, and directed him to go on and deliver it. The messenger did so, and Polysperchon sent the galley. Cassander, of course, watched for it, and seized it himself when it came. The last hope of the unhappy Olympias was thus extinguished, and she opened the gates and gave herself up to Cassander. The whole country immediately afterward fell into Cassander's hands.

The friends of the family of Antipater were now clamorous in their demands that Olympias should be brought to punishment for having so atrociously murdered the sons and relatives of Antipater while she was in power. Olympias professed herself willing to be tried, and appealed to the Macedonian senate to be her judges. She relied on the ascendency which she had so long exercised over the minds of the Macedonians, and did not believe that they would condemn her. Cassander himself feared that they would not; and although he was unwilling to murder her while she was a defenseless prisoner in his hands, he determined that she should die. He recommended to her secretly not to take the hazard of a trial, but to make her escape and go to Athens, and offered to give her an opportunity to do so. He intended, it was said, if she made the attempt, to intercept and slay her on the way as a fugitive from justice. She refused to accede to this proposal, suspecting, perhaps, Cassander's treachery in making it. Cassander then sent a band of two hundred soldiers to put her to death.

These soldiers, when they came into the prison, were so impressed by the presence of the queen, to whom, in former years, they had been accustomed to look up with so much awe, that they shrank back from their duty, and for a time it seemed that no one would strike the blow. At length, however, some among the number, who were relatives of those that Olympias had murdered, succeeding in nerving their arms with the resolution of revenge, fell upon her and killed her with their swords.

As for Roxana and the boy, Cassander kept them close prisoners for many years; and finally, feeling more and more that his possession of the throne of Alexander was constantly endangered by the existence of a son of Alexander, caused them to be assassinated too.

3

Early Life of Pyrrhus

B.C. 332-295

The family of Epirus.—Their difficulties.—The two Alexanders.—Their different destinies.—Adventures of Alexander of Macedon.—The Gulf of Tarentum.—Oracle of Dodona.—The equivocal prediction.—Pandosia. —The unexpected inundation.—Effects of it.—Bridge carried away. —The River of Sorrow.—Alexander killed.—His body falls into the river.—A woman rescues the remains.—Olympias.—Æacides marches to relieve Pydna.—The flight of the family with Pyrrhus.—The party meet with a narrow escape.—Ingenious mode of sending a letter.—The raft.— Pyrrhus is carried to Illyria.—Little Pyrrhus at the court of Glaucias.— Pyrrhus becomes a large boy.—Cassander's plans.—Glaucias establishes Pyrrhus on his throne.—Rebellion.—Pyrrhus once more an exile.— Pyrrhus enters into the service of Demetrius.—Pyrrhus acquires great renown.—He becomes a hostage.—The situation of a hostage.—Pyrrhus in the court of Ptolemy.

IN the two preceding chapters we have related that portion of the history of Macedonia which it is necessary to understand in order rightly to appreciate the nature of the difficulties in which the royal family of Epirus was involved at the time when Pyrrhus first appeared upon the stage. The sources of these difficulties were two: first, the uncertainty of the line of succession, there being two branches of the royal family, each claiming the throne, which state of things was produced, in a great measure, by the interposition of Olympias in the affairs of Epirus some years before; and, secondly, the act of Olympias in inducing Æacides to come to Macedonia, to embark in her quarrel against Cassander there. Of course, since there were two lines of princes, both claiming the throne, no sovereign of either line could hold any thing more than a divided empire over the hearts of his subjects; and consequently, when Æacides left the kingdom to fight the battles of Olympias in Macedon, it was comparatively easy for the party opposed to him to effect a revolution and raise their own prince to the throne.

The prince whom Olympias had originally made king of Epirus, to the exclusion of the claimant belonging to the other branch of the family, was her own brother. His name was Alexander. He was the son of Neoptolemus. The rival branch of the family were the children of Arymbas, the brother of Neoptolemus. This Alexander flourished at the same time as Alexander the Great, and in his character very much resembled his distinguished namesake. He commenced a career of conquest in Italy at the same time that his nephew embarked in his in Asia, and commenced it, too, under very similar circumstances. One went to the East, and another to the West, each determined to make himself master of the world. The Alexander of Macedon succeeded. The Alexander of Epirus failed. The one acquired, consequently, universal and perpetual renown, while the memory of the other has been almost entirely neglected and forgotten.

One reason, unquestionably, for the difference in these results was the difference in the character of the enemies respectively against whom the two adventurers had to contend. Alexander of Epirus went westward into Italy, where he had to encounter the soldiery of the Romans—a soldiery of the most rugged, determined, and indomitable character. Alexander of Macedon, on the other hand, went to the East, where he found only Asiatic races to contend with, whose troops, though countless in numbers and magnificently appointed in respect to all the purposes of parade and display, were yet enervated with luxury, and wholly unable to stand against any energetic and determined foe. In fact, Alexander of Epirus used to say that the reason why his nephew, Alexander of Macedon, had succeeded, while he himself had failed, was because he himself had invaded countries peopled by *men*, while the Macedonian, in his Asiatic campaign, had encountered only women.

However this may be, the campaign of Alexander of Epirus in Italy had a very disastrous termination. The occasion of his going there was a request which he had received from the inhabitants of Tarentum that he would come over and assist them in a war in which they were engaged with some neighboring tribes. Tarentum was a city situated toward the western shore of Italy. It was at the head of the deep bay called the Gulf of Tarentum, which bay occupies the hollow of the foot that the form of Italy presents to the eye as seen upon a map. Tarentum was, accordingly, across the Adriatic Sea from Epirus. The distance was about two hundred miles. By taking a southerly route, and going up the Gulf of Tarentum, this distance might be traversed wholly by sea. A little to the north the Adriatic is narrow, the passage there being only about fifty miles across. To an expedition, however, taking this course, there would remain, after arriving on the Italian shore, fifty miles or more to be accomplished by land in order to reach Tarentum.

Before deciding to comply with the request of the Tarentines that he would come to their aid, Alexander sent to a celebrated oracle in Epirus, called the oracle of Dodona, to inquire whether it would be safe for him to undertake the expedition. To his inquiries the oracle gave him this for an answer:

"The waters of Acheron will be the cause of your death, and Pandosia is the place where you will die."

Alexander was greatly rejoiced at receiving this answer. Acheron was a stream of Epirus, and Pandosia was a town upon the banks of it. He understood the response to mean that he was fated to die quietly in his own country at some future period, probably a remote one, and that there was no danger in his undertaking the expedition to which he had been called. He accordingly set sail from Epirus, and landed in Italy; and there, believing that he was fated to die in Epirus, and not in Italy, he fought in every battle with the most desperate and reckless bravery, and achieved prodigies of valor. The possibility that there might be an Acheron and a Pandosia in Italy, as well as in Epirus, did not occur to his mind.

For a time he was very successful in his career. He fought battles, gained victories, conquered cities, and established his dominion over quite an extended region. In order to hold what he had gained, he sent over a great number of hostages to Epirus, to be kept there as security for the continued submission of those whom he had subdued. These hostages consisted chiefly, as was usual in such cases, of children. At length, in the course of the war, an occasion arose in which it was necessary, for the protection of his troops, to encamp them on three hills which were situated very near to each other. These hills were separated by low interval lands and a small stream; but at the time when Alexander established his encampment, the stream constituted no impediment to free intercommunication between the different divisions of his army. There came on, however, a powerful rain; the stream overflowed its banks; the intervals were inundated. This enabled the enemy to attack two of Alexander's encampments, while it was utterly impossible for Alexander himself to render them any aid. The enemy made the attack, and were successful in it. The two camps were broken up, and the troops stationed in them were put to flight. Those that remained with Alexander, becoming discouraged by the hopeless condition in which they found themselves placed, mutinied, and sent to the camp of the enemy, offering to deliver up Alexander to them, dead or alive, as they should choose, on condition that they themselves might be allowed to return to their native land in peace. This proposal was accepted; but, before it was put in execution, Alexander, having discovered the plot, placed himself at the head of a determined and desperate band of followers, broke through the ranks of the enemies that surrounded him, and made his escape to a neighboring wood. From this wood he took a route which led him to a river, intending to pass the river by a bridge which he expected to find there, and then to destroy the bridge as soon as he had crossed it, so as to prevent his enemies from following him. By this means he hoped to make his way to some place of safety. He found, on arriving at the brink of the stream, that the bridge had been carried away by the inundation. He, however, pressed forward into the water on horseback, intending to ford the stream. The torrent was wild, and the danger was imminent, but Alexander pressed on. At length one of the attendants, seeing his master in imminent danger of being drowned, exclaimed aloud, "This cursed river! well is it named Acheron." The word Acheron, in the original language, signifies River of Sorrow.

By this exclamation Alexander learned, for the first time, that the river he was crossing bore the same name with the one in Epirus, which he supposed had been referred to in the warning of the oracle. He was at once overwhelmed with consternation. He did not know whether to go forward or to return. The moment of indecision was suddenly ended by a loud outcry from his attendants, giving the alarm that the traitors were close upon him. Alexander then pushed forward across the water. He succeeded in gaining the bank; but as soon as he did so, a dart from one of his enemies reached him and killed him on the spot. His lifeless body fell back into the river, and was floated down the stream, until at length it reached the camp of the enemy, which happened to be on the bank of the stream below. Here it was drawn out of the water, and subjected to every possible indignity. The soldiers cut the body in two, and, sending one part to one of the cities as a trophy of their victory, they set up the other part in the camp as a target for the soldiers to shoot at with darts and javelins.

At length a woman came into the camp, and, with earnest entreaties and many tears, begged the soldiers to give the mutilated corpse to her. Her object in wishing to obtain possession of it was, that she might send it home to Epirus, to the family of Alexander, and buy with it the liberty of her husband and her children, who were among the hostages which had been sent there. The soldiers acceded to this request, and the parts of the body having been brought together again, were taken to Epirus, and delivered to Olympias, by whom the remains were honorably interred. We must presume that the woman who sent them obtained the expected reward, in the return of her husband and children, though of this we are not expressly informed.

Of course, the disastrous result of this most unfortunate expedition had the effect, in Epirus, of diminishing very much the popularity and the strength of that branch of the royal family—namely, the line of Neoptolemus—to which Alexander had belonged. Accordingly, instead of being succeeded by one of his brothers, Æacides, the father of Pyrrhus, who was the representative of the other line, was permitted quietly to assume the crown. It might have been expected that Olympias would have opposed his accession, as she was herself a princess of the rival line. She did not, however, do so. On the contrary, she gave him her support, and allied herself to him very closely; and he, on his part, became in subsequent years one of her most devoted adherents and friends.

When Olympias was shut up in Pydna by the army of Cassander, as was related in the last chapter, and sent for Æacides to come to her aid, he immediately raised an army and marched to the frontier. He found the passes in the mountains which led from Epirus to Macedonia all strongly guarded, but he still determined to force his way through. He soon, however, began to observe marks of discontent and dissatisfaction among the officers of his army. These indications increased, until at length the disaffection broke out into open mutiny, as stated in the last chapter. Æacides then called his forces together, and gave orders that all who were unwilling to follow him into Macedon should be allowed freely to return. He did not wish, he said, that any should accompany him on such an expedition excepting those who went of their own free will. A considerable part of the army then returned, but, instead of repairing peaceably to their homes, they raised a general insurrection in Epirus, and brought the family of Neoptolemus again to the throne. A solemn decree of the state was passed, declaring that Æacides, in withdrawing from the kingdom, had forfeited his crown, and banishing him forever from the country. And as this revolution was intended to operate, not merely against Æacides personally, but against the branch of the royal family to which he belonged, the new government deemed it necessary, in order to finish their work and make it sure, that many of his relatives and friends, and especially his infant son and heir, should die. Several of the members of Æacides' family were accordingly killed, though the attendants in charge succeeded in saving the life of the child by a sudden flight.

The escape was effected by the instrumentality of two of the officers of Æacides' household, named Androclides and Angelus. These men, as soon as the alarm was given, hurried the babe away, with only such nurses and other attendants as it was necessary to take with them. The child was still unweaned; and though those in charge made the number of attendants as small as possible, still the party were necessarily of such a character as to forbid any great rapidity of flight. A troop was sent in pursuit of them, and soon began to draw near. When Androclides found that his party would be overtaken by the troop, he committed the child to the care of three young men, bidding them to ride on with him, at their utmost speed, to a certain town in Macedon, called Megaræ, where they thought he would be safe; and then he himself, and the rest of his company, turned back to meet the pursuers. They succeeded, partly by their representations and entreaties, and partly by such resistance and obstruction as it was in their power to make, in stopping the soldiers where they were. At length, having, though with some difficulty, succeeded in getting away from the soldiers, Androclides and Angelus rode on by secret ways till they overtook the three young men. They now began to think that the danger was over. At length, a little after sunset, they approached the town of Megaræ. There was a river just before the town, which looked too rough and dreadful to be crossed. The party, however, advanced to the brink, and attempted to ford the stream, but they found it impossible. It was growing dark; the water of the river, having been swelled by rains, was very high and boisterous, and they found that they could not get over. At length they saw some of the people of the town coming down to the bank on the opposite side. They were in hopes that these people could render them some assistance in crossing the stream, and they began to call out to them for this purpose; but the stream ran so rapidly, and the roaring of the torrent was so great, that they could not make themselves heard. The distance was very inconsiderable, for the stream was not wide; but, though the party with Pyrrhus called aloud and earnestly, and made signs, holding up the child in their arms to let the people see him, they could not make themselves understood.

At last, after spending some time in these fruitless efforts, one of the party who were with Pyrrhus thought of the plan of writing what they wished to say upon a piece of bark, and throwing it across the stream to those on the other side. They accordingly pulled off some bark from a young oak which was growing on a bank of the river, and succeeded in making characters upon it by means of the tongue of a buckle, sufficient to say that they had with them Pyrrhus, the young prince of Epirus, and that they were flying with him to save his life, and to implore the people on the other side to contrive some way to get them over the river. This piece of bark they then managed to throw across the stream. Some say that they rolled it around a javelin, and then gave the javelin to the strongest of their party to throw; others say that they attached it to a stone. In some way or other they contrived to give it a sufficient momentum to carry it across the water; and the people on the other side, when they obtained it, and read what was written upon it, were greatly excited by the tidings, and engaged at once with ardor and enthusiasm in efforts to save the child.

They brought axes and began to cut down trees to make a raft. In due time the raft was completed; and, notwithstanding the darkness of the night, and the force and swiftness of the current of the stream, the party of fugitives succeeded in crossing upon it, and thus brought the child and all the attendants accompanying him safely over.

The party with Pyrrhus did not intend to stop at Megaræ. They did not consider it safe, in fact, for them to remain in any part of Macedon, not knowing what course the war between Polysperchon and Cassander would take there, or how the parties engaged in the contest might stand affected toward Pyrrhus. They determined, therefore, to press forward in their flight till they had passed through Macedon, and reached the country beyond.

The country north of Macedon, on the western coast, the one in which they determined to seek refuge, was Illyria. The name of the King of Illyria was Glaucias. They had reason to believe that Glaucias would receive and protect the child, for he was connected by marriage with the royal family of Epirus, his wife, Beroa, being a princess of the line of Æacides. When the fugitives arrived at the court of Glaucias, they went to the palace, where they found Glaucias and Beroa; and, after telling the story of their danger and escape, they laid the child down as a suppliant at the feet of the king.

Glaucias felt not a little embarrassed at the situation in which he was placed, and did not know what to do. He remained for a long time silent. At length, little Pyrrhus, who was all the while lying at his feet, began to creep closer toward him; and, finally, taking hold of the king's robe, he began to climb up by it, and attempted to get into his lap, looking up into the king's face, at the same time, with a countenance in which the expression of confidence and hope was mingled with a certain instinctive infantile fear. The heart of the king was so touched by this mute appeal, that he took the child up in his arms, dismissed at once all prudential considerations from his mind, and, in the end, delivered the boy to the queen, Beroa, directing her to bring him up with her own children.

Cassander soon discovered the place of Pyrrhus's retreat, and he made great efforts to induce Glaucias to give him up. He offered Glaucias a very large sum of money if he would deliver Pyrrhus into his hands; but Glaucias refused to do it. Cassander would, perhaps, have made war upon Glaucias to compel him to comply with this requisition, but he was then fully occupied with the enemies that threatened him in Greece and Macedon. He did, subsequently, make an attempt to invade the dominions of Glaucias, and to get possession of the person of Pyrrhus, but the expedition failed, and after that the boy was allowed to remain in Illyria without any further molestation.

Time passed on, until at length Pyrrhus was twelve years old. During this interval great changes took place in the affairs of Cassander in Macedon. At first he was very successful in his plans. He succeeded in expelling Polysperchon from the country, and in establishing himself as king. He caused Roxana and the young Alexander to be assassinated, as was stated in the last chapter, so as to remove out of the way the only persons who he supposed could ever advance any rival claims to the throne. For a time every thing went well and prosperously with him, but at length the tide of his affairs seemed to turn. A new enemy appeared against him in Asia—a certain distinguished commander, named Demetrius, who afterward became one of the most illustrious personages of his age. Just at this time, too, the King of Epirus, Alcetus, the prince of the family of Neoptolemus, who had reigned during Pyrrhus's exile in Illyria, died. Glaucias deemed this a favorable opportunity for restoring Pyrrhus to the throne. He accordingly placed himself at the head of an army, and marched into Epirus, taking the young prince with him. No effectual resistance was made, and Pyrrhus was crowned king. He was, of course, too young actually to reign, and a sort of regent was accordingly established in power, with authority to govern the country in the young king's name until he should come of age.

This state of things could not be very stable. It endured about five years; and during this time Pyrrhus seemed to be very firmly established in power. The strength of his position, however, was more apparent than real; for the princes of the other branch of the family, who had been displaced by Pyrrhus's return to power, were of course discontented and restless all the time. They were continually forming plots and conspiracies, and were only waiting for an opportunity to effect another revolution. The opportunity at length came. One of the sons of Glaucias was to be married. Pyrrhus had been the companion and playmate of this prince during his residence in Illyria, and was, of course, invited to the wedding. Supposing that all was safe in his dominions, he accepted the invitation, and went to Illyria. While he was there, amusing himself in the festivities and rejoicings connected with the wedding, his rivals raised a rebellion, took possession of the government, and of all of Pyrrhus's treasures, killed or put to flight his partisans and friends, and raised a prince of the family of Neoptolemus to the throne. Pyrrhus found himself once more an exile.

The revolution in Epirus was so complete, that, after careful consideration and inquiry, Pyrrhus could see, with the resources he had at his command, no hope of recovering his throne. But, being of an ambitious and restless spirit, he determined not to remain idle; and he concluded, therefore, to enter into the service of Demetrius in his war against Cassander. There were two considerations which led him to do this. In the first place, Cassander was his most formidable enemy, and the prospect of his being ultimately restored again to his throne would depend almost entirely, he well knew, upon the possibility of destroying, or at least curtailing, Cassander's power. Then, besides, Demetrius was especially his friend. The wife of Demetrius was Deidamia, the sister of Pyrrhus, so that Pyrrhus looked upon Demetrius as his natural ally. He accordingly offered to enter the service of Demetrius, and was readily received. In fact, notwithstanding his youth—for he was now only seventeen or eighteen years of age—Demetrius gave him a very important command in his army, and took great pains to instruct him in the art of war. It was not long before an opportunity was afforded to make trial of Pyrrhus's capacity as a soldier. A great battle was fought at Ipsus, in Asia Minor, between Demetrius on one side and Cassander on the other. Besides these two commanders, there were many princes and generals of the highest rank who took part in the contest as allies of the principal combatants, which had the effect of making the battle a very celebrated one, and of causing it to attract very strongly the attention of all mankind at the time when it occurred. The result of the contest was, on the whole, unfavorable to the cause of Demetrius. His troops, generally, were compelled to give way, though the division which Pyrrhus commanded retained their ground. Pyrrhus, in fact, acquired great renown by his courage and energy, and perhaps still more by his success on this occasion. Young as he was, Demetrius immediately gave him a new and very responsible command, and intrusted to him the charge of several very important expeditions and campaigns, in all of which the young soldier evinced such a degree of energy and courage, combined, too, with so much forethought, prudence, and military skill, as presaged very clearly his subsequent renown.

At length an alliance was formed between Demetrius and Ptolemy, king of Egypt, and as security for the due execution of the obligations assumed by Demetrius in the treaty which they made, Ptolemy demanded a hostage. Pyrrhus offered to go himself to Egypt in this capacity. Ptolemy accepted him, and Pyrrhus was accordingly taken in one of Ptolemy's ships across the Mediterranean to Alexandria.

In Egypt the young prince was, of course, an object of universal attention and regard. He was tall and handsome in person, agreeable in manners, and amiable and gentle in disposition. His royal rank, the fame of the exploits which he had performed, the misfortunes of his early years, and the strange and romantic adventures through which he had passed, all conspired to awaken a deep interest in his favor at the court of Ptolemy. The situation of a hostage, too, is always one which strongly attracts the sympathy and kind feelings of those who hold him in custody. A captive is regarded in some sense as an enemy; and though his hard lot may awaken a certain degree of pity and commiseration, still the kind feeling is always modified by the fact that the object of it, after all, though disarmed and helpless, is still a foe. A hostage, however, is a friend. He comes as security for the faithfulness of a friend and an ally, so that the sympathy and interest which are felt for him as an exile from his native land, are heightened by the circumstance that his position makes him naturally an object of friendly regard.

The attachment which soon began to be felt for Pyrrhus in the court of Ptolemy was increased by the excellent conduct and demeanor which he exhibited while he was there. He was very temperate and moderate in his pleasures, and upright and honorable in all his doings. In a word, he made himself a general favorite; and after a year or two he married Antigone, a princess of the royal family. From being a hostage he now became a guest, and shortly afterward Ptolemy fitted out an expedition to proceed to Epirus and restore him to his throne. On arriving in Epirus, Pyrrhus found every thing favorable to the success of his plans. The people of the country had become discontented with the government of the reigning king, and were very willing to receive Pyrrhus in his place. The revolution was easily effected, and Pyrrhus was thus once more restored to his throne.

4

Wars in Macedon

B.C. 295-288

Pyrrhus is restored to his throne.—A celebration.—Festivities.—Gelon's gift.—Gelon and Myrtilus form a plot.—The cup-bearer pretends to join the plot.—Conversation overheard in a very singular manner.—Quarrel between Cassander's heirs.—Pyrrhus takes his first independent command.—Anecdotes of Pyrrhus.—His popularity.—Pyrrhus detects a forgery.—Plan of the forgers.—The war is ended.—Pyrrhus returns home.—Interview with Demetrius on the frontier.—Plots and counterplots.—Demetrius triumphs.—Relations between Demetrius and Pyrrhus.—War breaks out between them.—Thebes.—Recklessness and cruelty of Demetrius.—War between Pyrrhus and Demetrius.—Pantauchus.—The single combat.—Pyrrhus wounded.—Pantauchus narrowly escapes death.—Demetrius is hated by his subjects.—His famous garment.—It is left unfinished.—Pyrrhus's wives.—His motive for marrying Lanassa.—Lanassa is discontented, and deserts Pyrrhus.—War protracted for many years.

THE prince whom Pyrrhus displaced from the throne of Epirus on his return from Egypt, as narrated in the last chapter, was, of course, of the family of Neoptolemus. His own name was Neoptolemus, and he was the second son of the Neoptolemus who gave his name to the line.

Pyrrhus exercised an uncommon degree of moderation in his victory over his rival; for, instead of taking his life, or even banishing him from the kingdom, he treated him with respectful consideration, and offered, very generously, as it would seem, to admit him to a share of the regal power. Neoptolemus accepted this proposal, and the two kings reigned conjointly for a considerable time. A difficulty, however, before long occurred, which led to an open quarrel, the result of which was that Neoptolemus was slain. The circumstances, as related by the historians of the time, were as follows:

It seems that it was the custom of the people of Epirus to celebrate an annual festival at a certain city in the kingdom, for the purpose chiefly of renewing the oaths of allegiance on the one part, and of fealty on the other, between the people and the king. Of course, there were a great many games and spectacles, as well as various religious rites and ceremonies, connected with this celebration; and among other usages which prevailed, it was the custom for the people to bring presents to the king on the occasion. When the period for this celebration recurred, after Pyrrhus's restoration to the throne, both Pyrrhus and Neoptolemus, each attended by his own particular followers and friends, repaired to the city where the celebration was to be held, and commenced the festivities.

Among other donations which were made to Pyrrhus at this festival, he received a present of two yoke of oxen from a certain man named Gelon, who was a particular friend of Neoptolemus. It appears that it was the custom for the kings to dispose of many of the presents which they received on these occasions from the people of the country, by giving them to their attendants and the officers of their households; and a certain cup-bearer, named Myrtilus, begged Pyrrhus to give these oxen to him. Pyrrhus declined this request, but afterward gave the oxen to another man. Myrtilus was offended at this, and uttered privately many murmurings and complaints. Gelon, perceiving this, invited Myrtilus to sup with him. In the course of the supper, he attempted to excite still more the ill-will which Myrtilus felt toward Pyrrhus; and finding that he appeared to succeed in doing this, he finally proposed to Myrtilus to espouse the cause of Neoptolemus, and join in a plot for poisoning Pyrrhus. His office as cup-bearer would enable him, Gelon said, to execute such a design without difficulty or danger, and, by doing it, he would so commend himself to the regard of Neoptolemus, that he might rely on the most ample and abundant rewards. Myrtilus appeared to receive these proposals with great favor; he readily promised to embark in the plot, and promised to fulfill the part assigned him in the execution of it. When the proper time arrived, after the conclusion of the supper, Myrtilus took leave of Gelon, and, proceeding directly to Pyrrhus, he related to him all that had occurred.

Pyrrhus did not take any rash or hasty measures in the emergency, for he knew very well that if Gelon were to be then charged with the crime which he had proposed to commit, he would deny having ever proposed it, and that then there would be only the word of Myrtilus against that of Gelon, and that impartial men would have no positive means of deciding between them. He thought, therefore, very wisely, that, before taking any decided steps, it would be necessary to obtain additional proof that Gelon had really made the proposal. He accordingly directed Myrtilus to continue to pretend that he favored the plan, and to propose to Gelon to invite another cup-bearer, named Alexicrates, to join the plot. Alexicrates was to be secretly instructed to appear ready to enter into the conspiracy when he should be called upon, and thus, as Pyrrhus expected, the testimony of two witnesses would be obtained to Gelon's guilt.

It happened, however, that the necessary evidence against Gelon was furnished without a resort to this measure; for when Gelon reported to Neoptolemus that Myrtilus had acceded to his proposal to join him in a plan for removing Pyrrhus out of the way, Neoptolemus was so much overjoyed at the prospect of recovering the throne to his own family again, that he could not refrain from revealing the plan to certain members of the family, and, among others, to his sister Cadmia. At the time when he thus discovered the design to Cadmia, he supposed that nobody was within hearing. The conversation took place in an apartment where he had been supping with Cadmia, and it happened that there was a servant-woman lying upon a couch in the corner of the room at the time, with her face to the wall, apparently asleep. She was, in reality, not asleep, and she overheard all the conversation. She lay still, however, and did not speak a word; but the next day she went to Antigone, the wife of Pyrrhus, and communicated to her all that she had heard. Pyrrhus now considered the evidence that Neoptolemus was plotting his destruction as complete, and he determined to take decisive measures to prevent it. He accordingly invited Neoptolemus to a banquet. Neoptolemus, suspecting nothing, came, and Pyrrhus slew him at the table. Henceforward Pyrrhus reigned in Epirus alone.

Pyrrhus was now about twenty-three years of age, and inasmuch as, with all his moderation in respect to the pursuit of youthful pleasures, he was of a very ambitious and aspiring disposition, he began to form schemes and plans for the enlargement of his power. An opportunity was soon afforded him to enter upon a military career. Cassander, who had made himself King of Macedon in the manner already described, died about the time that Pyrrhus established himself on his throne in Epirus. He left two sons, Alexander and Antipater. These brothers immediately quarreled, each claiming the inheritance of their father's crown. Antipater proved to be the strongest in the struggle; and Alexander, finding that he could not stand his ground against his brother without aid, sent messengers at the same time to Pyrrhus, and also to Demetrius, in Thessaly, calling upon both to come to his assistance. They both determined to do so. Demetrius, however, was engaged in some enterprises which detained him for a time, but Pyrrhus immediately put himself at the head of his army, and prepared to cross the frontier.

The commencement of this march marks an important era in the life of Pyrrhus, for it was now for the first time that he had an army wholly under his command. In all the former military operations in which he had been engaged, he had been only a general, acting under the orders of his superiors. Now he was an independent sovereign, leading forth his own troops to battle, and responsible to no one for the manner in which he exercised his power. The character which he displayed in this new capacity was such as very soon to awaken the admiration of all his troops, and to win their affection in a very strong degree. His fine personal appearance, his great strength and dexterity in all martial exercises, his kind consideration for his soldiers, the systematic and skillful manner in which all his arrangements were made, and a certain nobleness and generosity of character which he displayed on many occasions, all combined to make him an object of universal favor and regard.

Various anecdotes were related of him in camp, which evinced the superiority of his mind, and that peculiar sense of confidence and strength which so often accompanies greatness. At one time a person was accused of being disaffected toward him, and of being in the habit of speaking evil of him on all occasions; and some of his counselors proposed that the offender should be banished. "No," said Pyrrhus; "let him stay here, and speak evil of me only to a few, instead of being sent away to ramble about and give me a bad character to all the world." At another time, some persons, when half intoxicated, at a convivial entertainment, had talked very freely in censure of something which Pyrrhus had done. They were called to account for it; and when asked by Pyrrhus whether it was true that they had really said such things, they replied that it was true. "And there is no doubt," they added, "that we should have said things a great deal worse if we had more wine." Pyrrhus laughed at this reply, and dismissed the culprits without any punishment. These, and other similar indications of the magnanimity which marked the general's character, made a great and very favorable impression upon the minds of all under his command.

Possessing thus, in a very high degree, the confidence and affection of his troops, Pyrrhus was able to inspire them with his own ardor and impetuosity when they came to engage in battle, and his troops were victorious in almost every conflict. Wherever he went, he reduced the country into subjection to Alexander, and drove Antipater before him.

He left garrisons of his own in the towns which he captured, so as to make his conquests secure, and in a short time the prospect seemed certain that Antipater would be expelled from the country, and Alexander placed upon the throne.

In this crisis of their affairs, some of the allies of Antipater conceived the design of circumventing their enemy by artifice, since it appeared that he was so superior to them in force. They knew how strong was his feeling of reverence and regard for Ptolemy, the King of Egypt, his father-in-law, and they accordingly forged a letter to him in Ptolemy's name, enjoining him to make peace with Antipater, and withdraw from Macedon. Antipater, the letter said, was willing to pay him three hundred talents of silver in consideration of his doing so, and the letter strongly urged him to accede to this offer, and evacuate the kingdom.

It was much less difficult to practice a successful deception of this kind in ancient days than it is now, for then writing was usually performed by scribes trained for the purpose, and there was therefore seldom any thing in the handwriting of a communication to determine the question of its authenticity. Pyrrhus, however, detected the imposition which was attempted in this case the moment that he opened the epistle. It began with the words, "King Ptolemy to King Pyrrhus, greeting;" whereas the genuine letters of Ptolemy to his son-in-law were always commenced thus: "The father to his son, greeting."

Pyrrhus upbraided the contrivers of this fraud in severe terms for their attempt to deceive him. Still, he entertained the proposition that they made, and some negotiations were entered into, with a view to an amicable settlement of the dispute. In the end, however, the negotiations failed, and the war was continued until Alexander was established on his throne. Pyrrhus then returned to his own kingdom. He received, in reward for his services in behalf of Alexander, a grant of that part of the Macedonian territory which lies upon the coast of the Adriatic Sea, north of Epirus; and thus peace was restored, and all things seemed permanently settled.

It will be recollected, perhaps, by the reader, that at the time that Alexander sent for Pyrrhus to assist him, he had also sent for Demetrius, who had been in former years the ally and friend of Pyrrhus. In fact, Deidamia, the sister of Pyrrhus, was Demetrius's wife. Demetrius had been engaged with the affairs of his own government at the time that he received this message, and was not then ready to grant the desired aid. But after a time, when he had settled his own affairs, he placed himself at the head of an army and went to Macedon. It was now, however, too late, and Alexander was sorry to learn that he was coming. He had already parted with a considerable portion of his kingdom to repay Pyrrhus for his aid, and he feared that Demetrius, if he were allowed to enter the kingdom, would not he satisfied without a good part of the remainder.

He accordingly advanced to meet Demetrius at the frontier. Here, at an interview which he held with him, he thanked him for his kindness in coming to his aid, but said that his assistance would now not be required. Demetrius said that it was very well, and so prepared to return. Alexander, however, as Demetrius afterward alleged, did not intend to allow him to withdraw, but formed a plan to murder him at a supper to which he designed to invite him. Demetrius avoided the fate which was intended for him by going away unexpectedly from the supper before Alexander had time to execute his plan. Afterward, Demetrius invited Alexander to a supper. Alexander came unarmed and unprotected, in order to set his guest an example of unconcern, in hopes that Demetrius would come equally defenseless to a second entertainment which he had prepared for him the next day, and at which he intended to adopt such measures that his guest should not be able by any possibility to escape. Demetrius, however, did not wait for the second attempt, but ordered his servants to kill Alexander, and all who were with him, while they were at *his* table. One of Alexander's men, when the attack was made upon them, said, as the soldiers of Demetrius were stabbing him, "You are too quick for us by just one day."

THE HISTORY OF PYRRHUS

The Macedonian troops, whom Alexander had brought with him to the frontier, when they heard of the murder of their king, expected that Demetrius would come upon them at once, with all his army, and cut them to pieces. But, instead of this, Demetrius sent them word that he did not intend them any harm, but wished, on the contrary, for an opportunity to explain and justify to them what he had done. He accordingly met them, and made a set harangue, in which he related the circumstances which led him to take the life of Alexander, and justified it as an act of self-defense. This discourse was received with great applause, and the Macedonian soldiers immediately hailed Demetrius king.

How far there was any truth in the charge which Demetrius brought against Alexander of intending to kill him, it is, of course, impossible to say. There was no evidence of the fact, nor could there be any evidence but such as Demetrius might easily fabricate. It is the universal justification that is offered in every age by the perpetrators of political crimes, that they were compelled to perform themselves the deeds of violence and cruelty for which they are condemned, in order to anticipate and preclude the performance of similar deeds on the part of their enemies.

Demetrius and Pyrrhus were now neighboring kings, and, from the friendly relations which had subsisted between them for so many years, it might, perhaps, be supposed that the two kingdoms which they respectively ruled would enjoy, from this time, a permanent and settled peace, and maintain the most amicable intercourse with each other. But the reverse was the fact. Contentions and quarrels arose on the frontiers. Each nation complained that the borderers of the other made inroads over the frontier. Demetrius and Pyrrhus gradually got drawn into these disputes. Unfortunately for the peace of the two countries, Deidamia died, and the strong band of union which she had formed between the two reigning families was sundered. In a word, it was not long before Pyrrhus and Demetrius came to open war.

The war, however, which thus broke out between Demetrius and Pyrrhus did not arise wholly from accidental collisions occurring on the frontiers. Demetrius was a man of the most violent and insatiable ambition, and wholly unscrupulous in respect to the means of gratifying the passion. Before his difficulties with Pyrrhus began, he had made expeditions southwardly into Greece, and had finally succeeded in reducing a large portion of that country to his sway. He, however, at one time, in the course of his campaigns in Greece, narrowly escaped a very sudden termination of his career. He was besieging Thebes, one of the principal cities of Greece, and one which was obstinately determined not to submit to him. In fact, the inhabitants of the city had given him some special cause of offense, so that he was excessively angry with them, and though for a long time he made very little progress in prosecuting the siege, he was determined not to give up the attempt. At one period, he was himself called away from the place for a time, to engage in some military duty demanding his attention in Thessaly, and during his absence he left his son to conduct the siege. On his return to Thebes, he found that, through the energetic and obstinate resistance which was made by the people of Thebes, great numbers of his men were continually falling—so much so, that his son began to remonstrate with him against allowing so great and so useless a slaughter to go on. "Consider," said he, "why you should expose so many of your valiant soldiers to such sure destruction, when—"

Here Demetrius, in a passion, interrupted him, saying, "Give yourself no concern about how many of the soldiers are killed. The more there are killed, the fewer you will have to provide subsistence for!"

The brutal recklessness, however, which Demetrius thus evinced in respect to the slaughter of his troops was not attended, as such a feeling often is, with any cowardly unwillingness to expose himself to danger. He mingled personally in the contests that took place about the walls of the city, and hazarded his own life as freely as he required his soldiers to hazard theirs. At length, on one occasion, a javelin thrown from the wall struck him in the neck, and, passing directly through, felled him to the ground. He was taken up for dead, and borne to his tent. It was there found, on examination, that no great artery or other vital part had been wounded, and yet in a very short time a burning fever supervened, and for some time the life of Demetrius was in imminent danger. He still, however, refused to abandon the siege. At length, he recovered from the effects of his wound, and, in the end, the city surrendered.

It was on the return of Demetrius to Macedon, after the close of his successful campaign in Greece, that the war between him and Pyrrhus broke out. As soon as it appeared that actual hostilities were inevitable, both parties collected an army and prepared for the conflict.

They marched to meet each other, Pyrrhus from Epirus, and Demetrius from Macedon. It happened, however, that they took different routes, and thus passed each other on the frontier. Demetrius entered Epirus, and found the whole country open and defenseless before him, for the military force of the country was all with Pyrrhus, and had passed into Macedon by another way. Demetrius advanced accordingly, as far as he chose, into Pyrrhus's territories, capturing and plundering every thing that came in his way.

Pyrrhus himself, on the other hand, met with quite a different reception. Demetrius had not taken all his army with him, but had left a large detachment under the command of a general named Pantauchus, to defend the country during his absence. Pyrrhus encountered Pantauchus as he entered Macedon, and gave him battle. A very hard-fought and obstinate conflict ensued. In the course of it, Pantauchus challenged Pyrrhus to single combat. He was one of the most distinguished of Demetrius's generals, being celebrated above all the officers of the army for his dexterity, strength, and courage; and, as he was a man of very high and ambitious spirit, he was greatly pleased with the opportunity of distinguishing himself that was now before him. He conceived that a personal encounter with so great a commander as Pyrrhus would add very much to his renown.

Pyrrhus accepted the challenge. The preliminary arrangements were made. The combatants came out into the field, and, as they advanced to the encounter, they hurled their javelins at each other before they met, and then rushed forward to a close and mortal combat with swords. The fight continued for a long time. Pyrrhus himself received a wound; but, notwithstanding this, he succeeded in bringing his antagonist to the ground, and would have killed him, had not the friends of Pantauchus rushed on and rescued him from the danger. A general battle between the two armies ensued, in which Pyrrhus was victorious. The army of Pantauchus was totally routed, and five thousand men were taken prisoners.

The Macedonian troops whom Pyrrhus thus defeated, instead of being maddened with resentment and anger against their conqueror, as it might have been expected they would be, were struck with a sentiment of admiration for him. They applauded his noble appearance and bearing on the field, and the feats of courage and strength which he performed. There was a certain stern and lofty simplicity in his air and demeanor which reminded them, as they said, of Alexander the Great, whom many of the old soldiers remembered. They compared Pyrrhus in these respects with Demetrius, their own sovereign, greatly to the disadvantage of the latter; and so strong was the feeling which was thus excited in Pyrrhus's favor, that it was thought at the time that, if Pyrrhus had advanced toward the capital with a view to the conquest of the country, the whole army would have gone over at once to his side, and that he might have made himself king of Macedon without any further difficulty or trouble. He did not do this, however, but withdrew again to Epirus when Demetrius came back into Macedonia. The Macedonians were by no means pleased to see Demetrius return.

In fact, Demetrius was beginning to be generally hated by all his subjects, being regarded by them all as a conceited and cruel tyrant. He was not only unscrupulously ambitious in respect to the dominions of his neighbors, but he was unjust and overbearing in his treatment of his own friends. Pyrrhus, on the other hand, was kind and courteous to his army, both to the officers and soldiers. He lived in habits of great simplicity, and shared the hardships as well as the toils of those who were under his command. He gave them, too, their share of the glory which he acquired, by attributing his success to their courage and fidelity. At one time, after some brilliant campaign in Macedon, some persons in his army compared his progress to the flight of an eagle. "If I am an eagle," said he in reply, "I owe it to you, for you are the wings by means of which I have risen so high."

Demetrius, on the other hand, treated the officers and men under his command with a species of haughtiness and disdain. He seemed to regard them as very far beneath him, and to take pleasure in making them feel his vast superiority. He was vain and foppish in his dress, expended great sums in the adornment of his person, decorating his robes and vestments, and even his shoes, with gold and precious stones. In fact, he caused the manufacture of a garment to be commenced which he intended should outvie in magnificence and in costly adornments all that had ever before been fabricated. This garment was left unfinished at the time of his death, and his successors did not attempt to complete it. They preserved it, however, for a very long time as a curiosity, and as a memorial of vanity and folly.

Demetrius, too, was addicted to many vices, being accustomed to the unrestrained indulgence of his appetites and propensities in every form. It was in part owing to these excesses that he became so hateful in manners and character, the habitual indulgence of his animal appetites and propensities having had the effect of making him morose and capricious in mind.

The hostility between Pyrrhus and Demetrius was very much increased and aggravated at one time by a difficulty in which a lady was concerned. Antigone, the first wife of Pyrrhus, died, and after her death Pyrrhus married two or three other wives, according to the custom which prevailed in those days among the Asiatic kings. Among these wives was Lanassa, the daughter of Agathocles, the king of Syracuse. The marriage of Pyrrhus with Antigone was apparently prompted by affection; but his subsequent alliances seem to have been simple measures of governmental policy, designed only to aid him in extending his dominions or strengthening his power. His inducement for marrying Lanassa was to obtain the island of Corcyra, which the King of Syracuse, who held that island at that time under his dominion, was willing to give to his daughter as her dowry. Now the island of Corcyra, as will be seen from the map, was off the coast of Epirus, and very near, so that the possession of it would add very considerably to the value of Pyrrhus's dominion.

Lanassa was not happy as Pyrrhus's bride. In fact, to have been married for the sake of an island brought as dowry, and to be only one of several wives after all, would not seem to be circumstances particularly encouraging in respect to the promise of conjugal bliss. Lanassa complained that she was neglected; that the other wives received attentions which were not accorded to her. At last, when she found that she could endure the vexations and trials of her condition no longer, she left her husband and went back to Corcyra, and then sent an invitation to Demetrius to come and take possession of the island, and marry her. In a word, she divorced herself and resumed possession of her dowry, and considered herself at liberty to dispose of both her person and her property anew.

Demetrius accepted the offer which was made him. He went to Corcyra, married Lanassa, and then, leaving a garrison to protect the island from any attempt which Pyrrhus might make to recover it, he went back to Macedon. Of course, after this transaction, Pyrrhus was more incensed against Demetrius than ever.

Very soon after this Pyrrhus had an opportunity to revenge himself for the injury which Demetrius had done him. Demetrius was sick; he had brought on a fever by excessive drinking. Pyrrhus determined to take advantage of the occasion to make a new invasion of Macedonia. He accordingly crossed the frontier at the head of a numerous army. Demetrius, sick as he was, mounted on horseback, and put himself at the head of his forces to go out to meet his enemy. Nothing important resulted from this campaign; but, after some ineffectual attempts at conquest, Pyrrhus returned to his own country.

In this way the war between Pyrrhus and Demetrius was protracted for many years, with varying success, one party being sometimes triumphant, and sometimes the other. At last, at a time when the tide of fortune seemed inclined to turn against Pyrrhus, some circumstances occurred which were the means of attracting his attention strongly in another direction, and ended in introducing him to a new and very brilliant career in an altogether different region. These circumstances, and the train of events to which they led, will form the subject of the following chapter.

* * *

Map—Grecian Empire

5

War in Italy

B.C. 280

The grand expedition into Italy.—The dominion of the Romans.—The Tarentines.—Various parties formed at Tarentum.—Boisterous meetings.—Meton's artifice.—Meton succeeds in accomplishing his aim.—Pyrrhus is invited to come to Tarentum.—Great numbers of volunteers.—Cineas.—Cineas propounds questions to Pyrrhus.—Pyrrhus explains his designs and plans.—The opinion of Cineas on the subject.—Pyrrhus sets sail.—His fleet and army.—Pyrrhus narrowly escapes death by shipwreck.—He establishes himself at Tarentum.—His energy.—Pyrrhus adopts very decisive measures.—The Tarentines were Greeks in origin.—Troops come in slowly.—Lævinus.—Pyrrhus sees a Roman encampment.—The Romans attack Pyrrhus by crossing the river.—Extraordinary spectacle.—Pyrrhus conspicuous.—Conversation between Pyrrhus and Leonatus.—Pyrrhus in dreadful danger.—The elephants.—Trophies borne through the field.—Pyrrhus shows himself.—The Romans defeated.

THE grand undertaking in which Pyrrhus now engaged, as indicated in the last chapter, the one in which he acquired such great renown, was an expedition into Italy against the Romans. The immediate occasion of his embarking in this enterprise was an invitation which he received from the inhabitants of Tarentum to come to their aid. His predecessor,

Alexander, had been drawn into Italy precisely in the same way; and we might have supposed that Pyrrhus would have been warned by the terrible fate which Alexander met with not to follow in his steps. But military men are never deterred from dangerous undertakings by the disasters which others have encountered in attempting them before. In fact, perhaps Pyrrhus was the more eager to try his fortune in this field on account of the calamitous result of his uncle's campaign. He was unwilling that his kingdom of Epirus should rest under the discredit of a defeat, and he was fired with a special ambition to show that he could overcome and triumph where others had been overborne and destroyed.

The dominion of the Romans had extended itself before this time over a considerable portion of Italy, though Tarentum, and the region of country dependent upon it, had not yet been subdued. The Romans were, however, now gradually making their way toward the eastern and southern part of Italy, and they had at length advanced to the frontiers of the Tarentine territory; and having been met and resisted there by the Tarentine troops, a collision ensued, which was followed by an open and general war. In the struggle, the Tarentines found that they could not maintain their ground against the Roman soldiery. They were gradually driven back; and now the city itself was in very imminent danger.

The difficulties in which the Tarentines were placed were greatly increased by the fact that there was no well-organized and stable government ruling in the city. The government was a sort of democracy in its form, and in its action it seems to have been a democracy of a very turbulent character—the questions of public policy being debated and decided in assemblies of the people, where it would seem that there was very little of parliamentary law to regulate the proceedings; and now the dangers which threatened them on the approach of the Romans distracted their councils more than ever, and produced, in fact, universal disorder and confusion throughout the city.

Various parties were formed, each of which had its own set of measures to urge and insist upon. Some were for submitting to the Romans, and thus allowing themselves to be incorporated in the Roman commonwealth; others were for persevering in their resistance to the last extremity. In the midst of these disputes, it was suggested by some of the counselors that the reason why they had not been able to maintain their ground against their enemies was, that they had no commander of sufficient predominance in rank and authority to concentrate their forces, and employ them in an efficient and advantageous manner; and they proposed that, in order to supply this very essential deficiency, Pyrrhus should be invited to come and take the command of their forces. This plan was strongly opposed by the more considerate and far-sighted of the people; for they well knew that when a foreign power was called in, in such a manner, as a temporary friend and ally, it almost always became, in the end, a permanent master. The mass of the people of the city, however, were so excited by the imminence of the immediate peril, that it was impossible to impress them with any concern for so remote and uncertain a danger, and it was determined that Pyrrhus should be called.

It was said that the meetings which were held by the Tarentines while these proceedings were in progress, were so boisterous and disorderly that, as often happens in democratic assemblies, the voices of those who were in the minority could not be heard; and that at last one of the public men, who was opposed to the plan of sending the invitation to Pyrrhus, resorted to a singular device in order to express his opinion. The name of this personage was Meton. The artifice which he adopted was this: he disguised himself as a strolling mountebank and musician, and then, pretending to be half intoxicated, he came into the assembly with a garland upon his head, a torch in his hand, and with a woman playing on a sort of flute to accompany him. On seeing him enter the assembly, the people all turned their attention toward him. Some laughed, some clapped their hands, and others called out to him to give them a song. Meton prepared to do so; and when, after much difficulty, silence was at length obtained, Meton came forward into the space that had been made for him, and, throwing off his disguise, he called out aloud, "Men of Tarentum! You do well in calling for a song, and in enjoying the pleasures of mirth and merriment while you may; for I warn you that you will see very little like mirth or merriment in Tarentum after Pyrrhus comes."

The astonishment which this sudden turn in the affair occasioned, was succeeded for a moment by a murmur of assent, which seemed to pass through the assembly; the good sense of many of the spectators being surprised, as it were, into an admission that the sentiment which Meton had so surreptitiously found means to express to them was true. This pause was, however, but momentary. A scene of violent excitement and confusion ensued, and Meton and the woman were expelled from the meeting without any ceremony.

The resolution of sending for Pyrrhus was confirmed, and embassadors were soon afterward dispatched to Epirus. The message which they communicated to Pyrrhus on their arrival was, that the Tarentines, being engaged in a war with the Romans, invited Pyrrhus to come and take command of their armies. They had *troops* enough, they said, and all necessary provisions and munitions of war. All that they now required was an able and efficient general; and if Pyrrhus would come over to them and assume the command, they would at once put him at the head of an army of twenty thousand horse and three hundred and fifty thousand foot soldiers.

It seems incredible that a state should have attained to such a degree of prosperity and power as to be able to bring such a force as this into the field, while under the government of men who, when convened for the consideration of questions of public policy in a most momentous crisis, were capable of having their attention drawn off entirely from the business before them by the coming in of a party of strolling mountebanks and players. Yet such is the account recorded by one of the greatest historians of ancient times.

Pyrrhus was, of course, very much elated at receiving this communication. The tidings, too, produced great excitement among all the people of Epirus. Great numbers immediately began to offer themselves as volunteers to accompany the expedition. Pyrrhus determined at once to embark in the enterprise, and he commenced making preparations for it on a very magnificent scale; for, notwithstanding the assurance which the Tarentines had given him that they had a very large body of men already assembled, Pyrrhus seems to have thought it best to take with him a force of his own.

As soon as a part of his army was ready, he sent them forward under the command of a distinguished general and minister of state, named Cineas. Cineas occupied a very high position in Pyrrhus's court. He was a Thessalian by birth. He had been educated in Greece, under Demosthenes, and he was a very accomplished scholar and orator as well as statesman. Pyrrhus had employed him in embassies and negotiations of various kinds from time to time, and Cineas had always discharged these trusts in a very able and satisfactory manner. In fact, Pyrrhus, with his customary courtesy in acknowledging his obligations to those whom he employed, used to say that Cineas had gained him more cities by his address than he had ever conquered for himself by his arms.

Cineas, it was said, was, in the outset, not much in favor of this expedition into Italy. The point of view in which he regarded such an enterprise was shown in a remarkable conversation which he held with Pyrrhus while the preparations were going on. He took occasion to introduce the subject one day, when Pyrrhus was for a short period at leisure in the midst of his work, by saying,

"The Romans are famed as excellent soldiers, and they have many warlike nations in alliance with them. But suppose we succeed in our enterprise and conquer them, what use shall we make of our victory?"

"Your question answers itself," replied the king. "The Romans are the predominant power in Italy. If they are once subdued, there will be nothing in Italy that can withstand us; we can go on immediately and make ourselves masters of the whole country."

After a short pause, during which he seemed to be reflecting on the career of victory which Pyrrhus was thus opening to view, Cineas added,

"And after we have conquered Italy, what shall we do next?"

"Why, there is Sicily very near," replied Pyrrhus, "a very fruitful and populous island, and one which we shall then very easily be able to subdue. It is now in a very unsettled state, and could do nothing effectual to resist us."

"I think that is very true," said Cineas; "and after we make ourselves masters of Sicily, what shall we do then?"

"Then," replied Pyrrhus, "we can cross the Mediterranean to Lybia and Carthage. The distance is not very great, and we shall be able to land on the African coast at the head of such a force that we shall easily make ourselves masters of the whole country. We shall then have so extended and established our power, that no enemy can be found in any quarter who will think of opposing us."

"That is very true," said Cineas; "and so you will then be able to put down effectually all your old enemies in Thessaly, Macedon, and Greece, and make yourself master of all those countries. And when all this is accomplished, what shall we do then?"

"Why, then," said Pyrrhus, "we can sit down and take our ease, and eat, drink, and be merry."

"And why," rejoined Cineas, "can not we sit down and take our ease, and enjoy ourselves now, instead of taking all this trouble beforehand? You have already at your command every possible means of enjoyment; why not make yourself happy with them now, instead of entering on a course which will lead to such dreadful toils and dangers, such innumerable calamities, and through such seas of blood, and yet bring you after all, at the end, nothing more than you have at the beginning?"

It may, perhaps, be a matter of doubt whether Cineas intended this as a serious remonstrance against the execution of Pyrrhus's designs, or only as an ingenious and good-humored satire on the folly of ambition, to amuse the mind of his sovereign in some momentary interval of leisure that came in the midst of his cares. However it may have been intended, it made no serious impression on the mind of Pyrrhus, and produced no change in his plans. The work of preparation went vigorously on; and as soon as a portion of the troops were ready to embark, Cineas was put in command of them, and they crossed the Adriatic Sea. After this, Pyrrhus completed the organization of the remaining force. It consisted of twenty elephants, three thousand horse, and twenty thousand foot, with two thousand archers, and twenty thousand slingers. When all was ready, Pyrrhus put these troops on board a large fleet of galleys, transports, and flat-bottomed boats, which had been sent over to him from Tarentum by Cineas for the purpose, and at length set sail. He left Ptolemy, his eldest son, then about fifteen years old, regent of the kingdom, and took two younger sons, Alexander and Helenus, with him. The expedition was destined, it seems, to begin in disaster; for no sooner had Pyrrhus set sail than a terrible storm arose, which, for a time, threatened the total destruction of the fleet, and of all who were on board of it. The ship which conveyed Pyrrhus himself was, of course, larger and better manned than the others, and it succeeded at length, a little after midnight, in reaching the Italian shore, while the rest of the fleet were driven at the mercy of the winds, and dispersed in every direction over the sea, far and wide. But, though Pyrrhus's ship approached the shore, the violence of the winds and waves was so great, that for a long time it was impossible for those on board to land. At length the wind suddenly changed its direction, and began to blow very violently off the shore, so that there seemed to be great probability that the ship would be driven to sea again. In fact, so imminent was the danger, that Pyrrhus determined to throw himself into the sea and attempt to swim to the shore. He accordingly did so, and was immediately followed by his attendants and guards, who leaped into the water after him, and did every thing in their power to assist him in gaining the land. The danger, however, was extreme; for the darkness of the night, the roaring of the winds and waves, and the violence with which the surf regurgitated from the shore, rendered the scene terrific beyond description. At last, however, about daybreak, the shipwrecked company succeeded in gaining the land.

Pyrrhus was almost completely exhausted in body by the fatigues and exposures which he had endured, but he appeared to be by no means depressed in mind. The people of the country flocked down to the coast to render aid. Several other vessels afterward succeeded in reaching the shore; and as the wind now rapidly subsided, the men on board of them found comparatively little difficulty in effecting a landing. Pyrrhus collected the remnant thus saved, and marshaled them on the shore. He found that he had about two thousand foot, a small body of horse, and two elephants. With this force he immediately set out on his march to Tarentum. As he approached the city, Cineas came out to meet him at the head of the forces which had been placed at his command, and which had made the passage in safety.

As soon as Pyrrhus found himself established in Tarentum, he immediately assumed the command of every thing there, as if he were already the acknowledged sovereign of the city. In fact, he found the city in so disorganized and defenseless a condition, that this assumption of power on his part seemed to be justified by the necessity of the case. The inhabitants, as is often the fact with men when their affairs are in an extreme and desperate condition, had become reckless. Every where throughout the city disorder and idleness reigned supreme. The men spent their time in strolling about from place to place, or sitting idly at home, or gathering in crowds at places of public diversion. They had abandoned all care or concern about public affairs, trusting to Pyrrhus to save them from the impending danger. Pyrrhus perceived, accordingly, that an entire revolution in the internal condition of the city was indispensably required, and he immediately took most efficient measures for effecting it. He shut up all the places of public amusement, and even the public walks and promenades, and put an end to all feastings, revels, and entertainments. Every man capable of bearing arms was enrolled in the army, and the troops thus formed were brought out daily for severe and long-protracted drillings and reviews. The people complained loudly of these exactions; but Pyrrhus had the power in his hands, and they were compelled to submit. Many of the inhabitants, however, were so dissatisfied with these proceedings, that they went away and left the city altogether. Of course it was those who were the most hopelessly idle, dissolute, and reckless that thus withdrew, while the more hardy and resolute remained. While these changes were going on, Pyrrhus set up and repaired the defenses of the city. He secured the walls, and strengthened the gates, and organized a complete system of guards and sentries. In a word, the condition of Tarentum was soon entirely changed. From being an exposed and defenseless town, filled with devotees of idleness and pleasure, it became a fortress, well secured at all points with material defenses, and occupied by a well-disciplined and resolute garrison.

The inhabitants of the southeastern part of Italy, where Tarentum was situated, were of Greek origin, the country having been settled, as it would seem, by emigrants from the opposite shores of the Adriatic Sea. Their language, therefore, as well as their customs and usages of life, were different from those of the Roman communities that occupied the western parts of the peninsula. Now the Greeks at this period regarded themselves as the only truly civilized people in the world; all other nations they called barbarians. The people of Tarentum, therefore, in sending for Pyrrhus to come to their aid against the Romans, did not consider him as a foreigner brought in to help them in a civil war against their own countrymen, but rather as a fellow-countryman coming to aid them in a war against foreigners. They regarded him as belonging to the same race and lineage with themselves, while the enemies who were coming from beyond the Apennines to assail them they looked upon as a foreign and barbarous horde, against whom it was for the common interest of all nations of Greek descent to combine. It was this identity of interest between Pyrrhus and the people whom he came to aid, in respect both to their national origin and the cause in which they were engaged, which made it possible for him to assume so supreme an authority over all their affairs when he arrived at Tarentum.

The people of the neighboring cities were slow in sending in to Pyrrhus the quotas of troops which the Tarentines had promised him;

and before his force was collected, the tidings arrived that the Romans were coming on at the head of a great army, under the command of the consul Lævinus. Pyrrhus immediately prepared to go forth to meet them. He marshaled the troops that were already assembled, and leaving the city, he advanced to meet the consul. After proceeding some way, he sent forward an embassador to the camp of Lævinus to propose to that general that, before coming to extremities, an effort should be made to settle the dispute between the Romans and Tarentines in some amicable manner, and offering his services as an umpire and mediator for this purpose. To this embassage Lævinus coolly replied "that he did not choose to accept Pyrrhus as a mediator, and that he did not fear him as an enemy." Of course, after receiving such a message as this, there was nothing left to Pyrrhus but to prepare for war.

He advanced, accordingly, at the head of his troops, until, at length, he reached a plain, where he encamped with all his forces. There was a river before him, a small stream called the River Siris. The Romans came up and encamped on the opposite side of the bank of this stream. Pyrrhus mounted his horse and rode to an eminence near the river to take a view of them.

He was much surprised at what he saw. The order of the troops, the systematic and regular arrangement of guards and sentinels, and the regularity of the whole encampment, excited his admiration.

"Barbarians!" said he. "There is certainly nothing of the barbarian in their manner of arranging their encampment, and we shall soon see how it is with them in other respects."

So saying, he turned away, and rode to his own camp. He, however, now began to be very seriously concerned in respect to the result of the approaching contest. The enemy with whom he was about to engage was obviously a far more formidable one than he had anticipated. He resolved to remain where he was until the allies whom he was expecting from the other Grecian cities should arrive. He accordingly took measures for fortifying himself as strongly as possible in his position, and he sent down a strong detachment from his main body to the river, to guard the bank and prevent the Romans from crossing to attack him. Lævinus, on the other hand, knowing that Pyrrhus was expecting strong re-enforcements, determined not to wait till they should come, but resolved to cross the river at once, notwithstanding the guard which Pyrrhus had placed on the bank to dispute the passage.

The Romans did not attempt to cross the stream in one body. The troops were divided, and the several columns advanced to the river and entered the water at different points up and down the stream, the foot-soldiers at the fords, where the water was most shallow, and the horsemen at other places—the most favorable that they could find. In this manner the whole river was soon filled with soldiers. The guard which Pyrrhus had posted on the bank found that they were wholly unable to withstand such multitudes; in fact, they began to fear that they might be surrounded. They accordingly abandoned the bank of the river, and retreated to the main body of the army.

Pyrrhus was greatly concerned at this event, and began to consider himself in imminent danger. He drew up his foot-soldiers in battle array, and ordered them to stand by their arms, while he himself advanced, at the head of the horsemen, toward the river. As soon as he came to the bank, an extraordinary spectacle presented itself to view. The surface of the stream seemed covered in every part with shields, rising a little above the water, as they were held up by the arms of the horsemen and footmen who were coming over. As fast as the Romans landed, they formed an array on the shore, and Pyrrhus, advancing to them, gave them battle.

The contest was maintained, with the utmost determination and fury on both sides, for a long time. Pyrrhus himself was very conspicuous in the fight, for he wore a very costly and magnificent armor, and so resplendent in lustre withal as to be an object of universal attention. Notwithstanding this, he exposed himself in the hottest parts of the engagement, charging upon the enemy with the most dauntless intrepidity whenever there was occasion, and moving up and down the lines, wherever his aid or the encouragement of his presence was most

THE HISTORY OF PYRRHUS

required. At length one of his generals, named Leonatus, rode up to him and said,

"Do you see, sire, that barbarian trooper, on the black horse with the white feet? I counsel you to beware of him. He seems to be meditating some deep design against you; he singles you out, and keeps his eye constantly upon you, and follows you wherever you go. He is watching an opportunity to execute some terrible design, and you will do well to be on your guard against him."

"Leonatus," said Pyrrhus, in reply, "we can not contend against our destiny, I know very well; but it is my opinion that neither that man, nor any other man in the Roman army that seeks an encounter with me, will have any reason to congratulate himself on the result of it."

He had scarcely spoken these words when he saw the horseman whom Leonatus had pointed out coming down upon him at full speed, with his spear grasped firmly in his hands, and the iron point of it aimed directly at Pyrrhus. Pyrrhus sprang immediately to meet his antagonist, bringing his own spear into aim at the same time. The horses met, and were both thrown down by the shock of the encounter. The friends of Pyrrhus rushed to the spot. They found both horses had been thrust through by the spears, and they both lay now upon the ground, dying. Some of the men drew Pyrrhus out from under his horse and bore him off the field, while others stabbed and killed the Roman where he lay.

Pyrrhus, having escaped this terrible danger, determined now to be more upon his guard. He supposed, in fact, that the Roman officers would be made furious by the death of their comrade, and would make the most desperate efforts to avenge him. He accordingly contrived to find an opportunity, in the midst of the confusion of the battle, to put off the armor which made him so conspicuous, by exchanging with one of his officers, named Megacles. Having thus disguised himself, he returned to the battle. He brought up the foot-soldiers and the elephants; and, instead of employing himself, as heretofore, in performing single feats of personal valor, he devoted all his powers to directing the arrangements of the battle, encouraging the men, and rallying them when they were for a time driven away from their ground.

The Trophies

By the exchange of armor which Pyrrhus thus made he probably saved his life; for Megacles, wherever he appeared after he had assumed the dress of Pyrrhus, found himself always surrounded by enemies, who pressed upon him incessantly and every where in great numbers, and he was finally killed. When he fell, the men who slew him seized the glittering helmet and the resplendent cloak that he wore, and bore them off in triumph into the Roman lines, as proof that Pyrrhus was slain. The tidings, as it passed along from rank to rank of the army, awakened a long and loud shout of acclamation and triumph, which greatly excited and animated the Romans, while it awakened in the army of Pyrrhus a correspondent emotion of discouragement and fear. In fact, for a short time it was universally believed in both armies that Pyrrhus was dead. In order to correct this false impression among his own troops, which threatened for a season to produce the most fatal effects, Pyrrhus rode along the ranks with his head uncovered, showing himself to his men, and shouting to them that he was yet alive.

At length, after a long and very obstinate conflict, the Greeks gained the victory. This result was due in the end, in a great measure, to the elephants which Pyrrhus brought into the battle. The Roman horses, being wholly unused to the sight of such huge beasts, were terrified beyond measure at the spectacle, and fled in dismay whenever they saw the monsters coming. In fact, in some cases, the riders lost all command of their horses, and the troop turned and fled, bearing down and overwhelming the ranks of their friends behind them. In the end the Romans were wholly driven from the field. They did not even return to their camp, but, after recrossing the river in confusion, they fled in all directions, abandoning the whole country to their conqueror. Pyrrhus then advanced across the river and took possession of the Roman camp.

6

Negotiations

B.C. 280-279

Effects of the victory.—Public opinion at Rome.—Expectations of Pyrrhus. —His mistake.—Cineas sent an embassador to Rome.—Cineas's plans for bribing the Roman senators.—Speech of Cineas in the Roman senate.— Debate in the senate.—An incident of the discussion.—Appius Claudius is brought on a bed to the senate.—Speech of Appius Claudius.—Effect of his speech on the senate.—Cineas makes report of his mission.—Fabricius sent to Pyrrhus.—His reception.—The elephant concealed in the tent.— Pyrrhus makes great offers to Fabricius.—The Roman armies advance. —The two generals.—The armies encamp in sight of each other.—His military honors.—Story of Decius Mus.—The vision.—Extraordinary alternative proposed.—The two consuls draw lots.—Decius sacrifices himself.—Superstitious fears of the soldiers.—Decius Mus.—Reply of Decius Mus to Pyrrhus.—The Romans afraid of the elephants.—The battle.— The elephants.—War chariots.—Doubtful victory.—Winter- quarters.— Nicias.—Pyrrhus's physician.—His treachery.—A generous exchange of prisoners.—No peace.

THE result of the battle on the banks of the Siris, decisive and complete as the victory was on the part of the Greeks, produced, of course, a very profound sensation at Rome. Instead, however, of discouraging and disheartening the Roman senate and people, it only aroused them to fresh energy and determination. The victory was considered as wholly due to the extraordinary military energy and skill of Pyrrhus, and not to any superiority of the Greek troops over those of the Romans in courage, in discipline, or in efficiency in the field. In fact, it was a saying at Rome at the time, that it was Lævinus that had been conquered by Pyrrhus in the battle, and not the Romans by the Greeks. The Roman government, accordingly, began immediately to enlist new recruits, and to make preparations for a new campaign, more ample and complete, and on a far greater scale than before.

Pyrrhus was much surprised when he heard these things. He had supposed that the Romans would have been disheartened by the defeat which they had sustained, and would now think only of proposals and negotiations for peace. He seems to have been but very imperfectly informed in respect to the condition of the Roman commonwealth at this period, and to the degree of power to which it had attained. He supposed that, after suffering so signal and decisive a defeat, the Romans would regard themselves as conquered, and that nothing remained to them now but to consider how they could make the best terms with their conqueror. The Roman troops had, indeed, withdrawn from the neighborhood of the place where the battle had been fought, and had left Pyrrhus to take possession of the ground without molestation. Pyrrhus was even allowed to advance some considerable distance toward Rome; but he soon learned that, notwithstanding their temporary reverses, his enemies had not the most remote intention of submitting to him, but were making preparations to take the field again with a greater force than ever.

Under these circumstances, Pyrrhus was for a time somewhat at a loss what to do. Should he follow up his victory, and advance boldly toward the capital, with a view of overcoming the Roman power entirely, or should he be satisfied with the advantage which he had already gained, and be content, for the present, with being master of Western Italy? After much hesitation, he concluded on the latter course.

He accordingly suspended his hostile operations, and prepared to send an embassador to Rome to propose peace. Cineas was, of course, the embassador commissioned to act on this occasion.

Cineas accordingly proceeded to Rome. He was accompanied by a train of attendants suitable to his rank as a royal embassador, and he took with him a great number of costly presents to be offered to the leading men in Rome, by way, as it would seem, of facilitating his negotiations. The nature of the means which he thus appears to have relied upon in his embassy to Rome may, perhaps, indicate the secret of his success in the diplomatic duties which he had performed in Greece and in Asia, where he had acquired so much distinction for his dexterity in negotiating treaties favorable to the interests of his master. However this may be, Cineas found that the policy which he contemplated would not answer in Rome. Soon after his arrival in the city, and in an early stage of the negotiations, he began to offer his presents to the public men with whom he had to deal; but they refused to accept them. The Roman senators to whom the gifts were offered returned them all, saying that, in case a treaty should be concluded, and peace made between the two nations, they should then have no objections to an interchange of such civilities; but, while the negotiations were pending, they conceived it improper for them to receive any such offerings. It may, perhaps, be taken as an additional proof of the nature of the influences which Cineas was accustomed to rely upon in his diplomatic undertakings, that he offered many of his gifts on this occasion to the ladies of the Roman senators as well as to the senators themselves; but the wives were found as incorruptible as the husbands. The gifts were all alike returned.

Not discouraged by the failure of this attempt, Cineas obtained permission of the Roman senate to appear before them, and to address them on the subject of the views which Pyrrhus entertained in respect to the basis of the peace which he proposed. On the appointed day Cineas went to the senate-chamber, and there made a long and very able and eloquent address, in the presence of the senate and of the principal inhabitants of the city. He was very much impressed on this occasion with the spectacle which the august assembly presented to his view. He said afterward, in fact, that the Roman senate seemed to him like a congress of kings, so dignified and imposing was the appearance of the body, and so impressive was the air of calmness and gravity which reigned in their deliberations. Cineas made a very able and effective speech. He explained the views and proposals of Pyrrhus, presenting them in a light as favorable and attractive as possible. Pyrrhus was willing, he said, to make peace on equal terms. He proposed that he should give up all his prisoners without ransom, and that the Romans should give up theirs. He would then form an alliance with the Romans, and aid them in the future conquests that they meditated. All he asked was that he might have the sanction of the Roman government to his retaining Tarentum and the countries connected with and dependent upon it; and that, in maintaining his dominion over these lands, he might look upon the Roman people as his allies and friends.

After Cineas had concluded his speech and had withdrawn from the senate-chamber, a debate arose among the senators on the propositions which he had made to them. There was a difference of opinion; some were for rejecting the proposals at once; others thought that they ought to be accepted. Those who were inclined to peace urged the wisdom of acceding to Pyrrhus's proposals by representing the great danger of continuing the war. "We have already," said they, "lost one great and decisive battle; and, in case of the renewal of the struggle, we must expect to find our enemy still more formidable than he was before; for many of the Italian nations of the eastern coast have joined his standard since hearing of the victory which he has obtained, and more are coming in. His strength, in fact, is growing greater and greater every day; and it is better for us to make peace with him now, on the honorable terms which he proposes to us, rather than to risk another battle, which may lead to the most disastrous consequences."

In the midst of this discussion, an aged senator, who had been for a long time incapacitated by his years and infirmities from appearing in his seat, was seen coming to the assembly, supported and led by his sons and sons-in-law, who were making way for him in the passages and conducting him in. His name was Appius Claudius. He was blind and almost helpless through age and infirmity. He had heard in his chamber of the irresolution of the senate in respect to the further prosecution of the war with Pyrrhus, and had caused himself to be taken from his bed and borne through the streets by servants on a chair to the senate-house, that he might there once more raise his voice to save, if possible, the honor and dignity of his country. As he entered the chamber, he became at once the object of universal attention. As soon as he reached his seat, a respectful silence began to prevail throughout the assembly, all listening to hear what he had to say. He expressed himself as follows:

"Senators of Rome,—I am blind, and I have been accustomed to consider my blindness as a calamity; but now I could wish that I had been deaf as well as blind, and then I might never have heard of the disgrace which seems to impend over my country. Where are now the boastings that we made when Alexander the Great commenced his career, that if he had turned his arms toward Italy and Rome, instead of Persia and the East, we would never have submitted to him; that he never would have gained the renown of being invincible if he had only attacked *us*, but would, on the other hand, if he invaded our dominions, only have contributed to the glory of the Roman name by his flight or his fall? These boasts we made so loudly that the echo of them spread throughout the world. And yet now, here is an obscure adventurer who has landed on our shores as an enemy and an invader, and because he has met with a partial and temporary success, you are debating whether you shall not make an ignominious peace with him, and allow him to remain. How vain and foolish does all our boastful defiance of Alexander appear when we now tremble at the name of Pyrrhus—a man who has been all his life a follower and dependent of one of Alexander's inferior generals—a man who has scarcely been able to maintain himself in his own dominions—who could not retain even a small and insignificant part of Macedon which he had conquered, but was driven ignominiously from it; and who comes into Italy now rather as a refugee than a conqueror—an adventurer who seeks power here because he can not sustain himself at home! I warn you not to expect that you can gain any thing by making such a peace with him as he proposes. Such a peace makes no atonement for the past, and it offers no security for the future. On the contrary, it will open the door to other invaders, who will come, encouraged by Pyrrhus's success, and emboldened by the contempt which they will feel for you in allowing yourselves to be thus braved and insulted with impunity."

The effect of this speech on the senate was to produce a unanimous determination to carry on the war. Cineas was accordingly dismissed with this answer: that the Romans would listen to no propositions for peace while Pyrrhus remained in Italy. If he would withdraw from the country altogether, and retire to his own proper dominions, they would then listen to any proposals that he might make for a treaty of alliance and amity. So long, however, as he remained on Italian ground, they would make no terms with him whatever, though he should gain a thousand victories, but would wage war upon him to the last extremity.

Cineas returned to the camp of Pyrrhus, bearing this reply. He communicated also to Pyrrhus a great deal of information in respect to the government and the people of Rome, the extent of the population, and the wealth and resources of the city; for while he had been engaged in conducting his negotiations, he had made every exertion to obtain intelligence on all these points, and he had been a very attentive and sagacious observer of all that he had seen. The account which he gave was very little calculated to encourage Pyrrhus in his future hopes and expectations. The people of Rome, Cineas said, were far more numerous than he had before supposed. They had now already on foot an army twice as large as the one which Pyrrhus had defeated, and multitudes besides were still left in the city, of a suitable age for enlisting, sufficient to form even larger armies still. The prospect, in a word, was very far from such as to promise Pyrrhus an easy victory.

Of course, both parties began now to prepare vigorously for war. Before hostilities were resumed, however, the Romans sent a messenger to the camp of Pyrrhus to negotiate an exchange of prisoners. The name of this embassador was Fabricius. Fabricius, as Pyrrhus was informed by Cineas, was very highly esteemed at Rome for his integrity and for his military abilities, but he was without property, being dependent wholly on his pay as an officer of the army. Pyrrhus received Fabricius in the most respectful manner, and treated him with every mark of consideration and honor. He, moreover, offered him privately a large sum of money in gold. He told Fabricius that, in asking his acceptance of such a gift, he did not do it for any base purpose, but intended it only as a token of friendship and hospitality. Fabricius, however, refused to accept the present, and Pyrrhus pressed him no further.

The next day Pyrrhus formed a plan for giving his guest a little surprise. He supposed that he had never seen an elephant, and he accordingly directed that one of the largest of these animals should be placed secretly behind a curtain, in an apartment where Fabricius was to be received. The elephant was covered with his armor, and splendidly caparisoned. After Fabricius had come in, and while he was sitting in the apartment wholly unconscious of what was before him, all at once the curtain was raised, and the elephant was suddenly brought to view; and, at the same instant, the huge animal, raising his trunk, flourished it in a threatening manner over Fabricius's head, making at the same time a frightful cry, such as he had been trained to utter for the purpose of striking terror into the enemy, in charging upon them on the field of battle. Fabricius, instead of appearing terrified, or even astonished at the spectacle, sat quietly in his seat, to all appearance entirely unmoved, and, turning to Pyrrhus with an air of the utmost composure, said coolly, "You see that you make no impression upon me, either by your gold yesterday or by your beast to-day."

THE HISTORY OF PYRRHUS

The Elephant Concealed

Pyrrhus was not at all displeased with this answer, blunt as it may seem. On the contrary, he seems to have been very deeply impressed with a sense of the stern and incorruptible virtue of Fabricius's character, and he felt a strong desire to obtain the services of such an officer in his own court and army. He accordingly made new proposals to Fabricius, urging him to use his influence to induce the Romans to make peace, and then to go with him to Epirus, and enter into his service there.

"If you will do so," said Pyrrhus, "I will make you the chief of my generals, and my own most intimate friend and companion, and you shall enjoy abundant honors and rewards."

"No," replied Fabricius, "I can not accept those offers, nor is it for your interest that I should accept them; for, were I to go with you to Epirus, your people, as soon as they came to know me well, would lose all their respect for you, and would wish to have me, instead of you, for their king."

We are, perhaps, to understand this rejoinder, as well as the one which Fabricius made to Pyrrhus in respect to the elephant, as intended in a somewhat jocose and playful sense; since, if we suppose them to have been gravely and seriously uttered, they would indicate a spirit of vanity and of empty boasting which would seem to be wholly inconsistent with what we know of Fabricius's character. However this may be, Pyrrhus was pleased with both; and the more that he saw and learned of the Romans, the more desirous he became of terminating the war and forming an alliance with them. But the Romans firmly persisted in refusing to treat with him, except on the condition of his withdrawing first entirely from Italy, and this was a condition with which he deemed it impossible to comply. It would be equivalent, in fact, to an acknowledgment that he had been entirely defeated. Accordingly, both sides began again to prepare vigorously for war.

The Romans marched southward from the city with a large army, under the command of their two consuls. The names of the consuls at this time were Sulpicius Saverrio and Decius Mus. These generals advanced into Apulia, a country on the western coast of Italy, north of Tarentum. Here they encamped on a plain at the foot of the Apennines, near a place called Asculum. There was a stream in front of their camp, and the mountains were behind it. The stream was large and deep, and of course it greatly protected their position. On hearing of the approach of the Romans, Pyrrhus himself took the field at the head of all his forces, and advanced to meet them. He came to the plain on which the Roman army was encamped, and posted himself on the opposite bank of the stream. The armies were thus placed in close vicinity to each other, being separated only by the stream. The question was, which should attempt to cross the stream and make the attack upon the other. They remained in this position for a considerable time, neither party venturing to attempt the passage.

While things were in this condition—the troops on each side waiting for an opportunity of attacking their enemies, and probably without any fear whatever of the physical dangers which they were to encounter

THE HISTORY OF PYRRHUS

in the conflict—the feeling of composure and confidence among the men in Pyrrhus's army was greatly disturbed by a singular superstition. It was rumored in the army that Decius Mus, the Roman commander, was endowed with a species of magical and supernatural power, which would, under certain circumstances, be fatal to all who opposed him. And though the Greeks seem to have had no fear of the material steel of the Roman legions, this mysterious and divine virtue, which they imagined to reside in the commander, struck them with an invincible terror.

The story was, that the supernatural power in question originated in one of the ancestors of the present Decius, a brave Roman general, who lived and flourished in the century preceding the time of Pyrrhus. His name, too, was Decius Mus. In the early part of his life, when he was a subordinate officer, he was the means of saving the whole army from most imminent danger, by taking possession of an eminence among the mountains, with the companies that were under his command, and holding it against the enemy until the Roman troops could be drawn out of a dangerous defile where they would otherwise have been overwhelmed and destroyed. He was greatly honored for this exploit. The consul who commanded on the occasion rewarded him with a golden crown, a hundred oxen, and a magnificent white bull, with gilded horns. The common soldiers, too, held a grand festival and celebration in honor of him, in which they crowned him with a wreath made of dried grasses on the field, according to an ancient custom which prevailed among the Romans of rewarding in this way any man who should be the means of saving an army. Of course, such an event as saving an army was of very rare occurrence; and, accordingly, the crowning of a soldier by his comrades on the field was a very distinguished honor, although the decoration itself was made of materials so insignificant and worthless.

Decius rose rapidly after this time from rank to rank, until at length he was chosen consul. In the course of his consulship, he took the field with one of his colleagues, whose name was Torquatus, at the head of a large army, in the prosecution of a very important war in the interior of the country. The time arrived at length for a decisive battle to be fought. Both armies were drawn up on the field, the preparations were all made, and the battle was to be fought on the following day. In the night, however, a vision appeared to each consul, informing him that it had been decreed by fate that a *general* on one side and the *army* on the other were to be destroyed on the following day; and that, consequently, either of the consuls, by sacrificing himself, might secure the destruction of the enemy. On the other hand, if they were to take measures to save themselves, the general on the other side would be killed, and on their side the *army* would be defeated and cut to pieces.

The two consuls, on conferring together upon the following morning, immediately decided that either one or the other of them should die, in order to secure victory to the arms of their country; and the question at once arose, what method they should adopt to determine which of them should be the sacrifice. At last it was agreed that they would go into battle as usual, each in command of his own wing of the army, and that the one whose wing should first begin to give way should offer himself as the victim. The arrangements were made accordingly, and the result proved that Decius was the one on whom the dire duty of self-immolation was to devolve. The wing under his command began to give way. He immediately resolved to fulfill his vow. He summoned the high priest. He clothed himself in the garb of a victim about to be offered in sacrifice. Then, with his military cloak wrapped about his head, and standing upon a spear that had been previously laid down upon the ground, he repeated in the proper form words by which he devoted himself and the army of the enemy to the God of Death, and then finally mounted upon his horse and drove furiously in among the thickest of the enemy. Of course he was at once thrust through with a hundred spears and javelins; and immediately afterward the army of the enemy gave way on all hands, and the Romans swept the field, completely victorious.

The power which was in this instance supernaturally granted to Decius to secure the victory to the Roman arms, by sacrificing his own life on the field of battle, afterward descended, it was supposed, as an inheritance, from father to son. Decius Mus, the commander opposed to Pyrrhus, was the grandson of his namesake referred to above; and now it was rumored among the Greeks that he intended, as soon as the armies came into action, to make the destruction of his enemies sure by sacrificing himself, as his grandfather had done. The soldiers of Pyrrhus were willing to meet any of the ordinary and natural chances and hazards of war; but, where the awful and irresistible decrees of the spiritual world were to be against them, it is not strange that they dreaded the encounter.

Under these circumstances, Pyrrhus sent a party of messengers to the Roman camp to say to Decius, that if in the approaching battle he attempted to resort to any such arts of necromancy to secure the victory to the Roman side, he would find himself wholly unsuccessful in the attempt; for the Greek soldiers had all been instructed not to kill him if he should throw himself among them, but to take him alive and bring him a prisoner to Pyrrhus's camp; and that then, after the battle was over, he should be subjected, they declared, to the most cruel and ignominious punishments, as a magician and an impostor. Decius sent back word, in reply, that Pyrrhus had no occasion to give himself any uneasiness in respect to the course which the Roman general would pursue in the approaching battle. The measure that he had referred to was one to which the Romans were not accustomed to resort except in emergencies of the most extreme and dangerous character, and Pyrrhus ought not to flatter himself with the idea that the Romans regarded his invasion as of sufficient consequence to require them to have recourse to any unusual means of defense. They were fully convinced of their ability to meet and conquer him by ordinary modes of warfare. To prove that they were honest in this opinion, they offered to waive the advantage which the river afforded them as a means of defense, and allow Pyrrhus to cross it without molestation, with a view to fighting the battle afterward upon the open field; or they would themselves cross the river, and fight the battle on Pyrrhus's side of it—whichever Pyrrhus himself preferred.

They asked for no advantage, but were willing to meet their adversaries on equal terms, and abide by the result.

Pyrrhus could not with honor decline to accept this challenge. He decided to remain where he was, and allow the Romans to cross the stream. This they accordingly did; and when all the troops had effected the passage, they were drawn up in battle array on the plain. Pyrrhus marshaled his forces also, and both parties prepared for the contest.

The Romans stood most in awe of the elephants, and they resorted to some peculiar and extraordinary means of resisting them. They prepared a great number of chariots, each of which was armed with a long pointed spear, projecting forward in such a manner that when the chariots should be driven on toward the elephants, these spears or beaks should pierce the bodies of the beasts and destroy them. The chariots, too, were filled with men, who were all provided with fire-brands, which they were to throw at the elephants, and frighten them, as they came on. These chariots were all carefully posted in front of that part of Pyrrhus's army where the elephants were stationed, and the charioteers were strictly ordered not to move until they should see the elephants advancing.

The battle, as might have been expected from the circumstances which preceded it, and from the character of the combatants, was fought with the most furious and persevering desperation. It continued through the whole day; and in the various parts of the field, and during the different hours of the day, the advantage was sometimes strongly on one side, and sometimes on the other, so that it was wholly uncertain, for a long time, what the ultimate result would be. The elephants succeeded in getting round the chariots which had been posted to intercept them, and effected a great destruction of the Roman troops. On the other hand, a detachment of the Roman army made their way to the camp of Pyrrhus, and attacked it desperately. Pyrrhus withdrew a part of his forces to protect his camp, and that turned the tide against him on the field. By means of the most Herculean exertions, Pyrrhus rallied his men, and restored their confidence; and then, for a time, the fortune of war seemed to incline in his favor. In the course of the day Decius was killed, and the whole command of the Roman army then devolved upon Sulpicius, his colleague. Pyrrhus himself was seriously wounded. When, at last, the sun went down, and the approaching darkness of the night prevented a continuance of the combat, both parties drew off such as remained alive of their respective armies, leaving the field covered with the dead and dying. One of Pyrrhus's generals congratulated him on his victory. "Yes," said Pyrrhus; "another such victory, and I shall be undone."

In fact, after trying their strength against each other in this battle, neither party seemed to be in haste to bring on another contest. They both drew away to places of security, and began to send for re-enforcements, and to take measures to strengthen themselves for future operations. They remained in this state of inaction until at length the season passed away, and they then went into winter-quarters, each watching the other, but postponing, by common consent, all active hostilities until spring. In the spring they took the field again, and the two armies approached each other once more. The Roman army had now two new commanders, one of whom was the celebrated Fabricius, whom Pyrrhus had negotiated with on former occasions. The two commanders were thus well acquainted with each other; and though, as public men, they were enemies, in private and personally they were very good friends.

Pyrrhus had a physician in his service named Nicias. This man conceived the design of offering to the Romans to poison his master on condition of receiving a suitable reward. He accordingly wrote a letter to Fabricius making the proposal. Fabricius immediately communicated the letter to his colleague, and they both concurred in the decision to inform Pyrrhus himself of the offer which had been made them, and put him on his guard against the domestic traitor. They accordingly sent him the letter which they had received, accompanied by one from themselves, of the following tenor:

"Caius Fabricius and Quintus Æmilius to King Pyrrhus, greeting:

"You seem to be as unfortunate in the choice of your friends as you are in that of your enemies. The letter which we send herewith will satisfy you that those around you, on whom you rely, are wholly unworthy of your confidence. You are betrayed; your very physician, the man who ought to be most faithful to you, offers to poison you. We give you this information, not out of any particular friendship for you, but because we do not wish to be suspected of conniving at an assassination—a crime which we detest and abhor. Besides, we do not wish to be deprived of the opportunity of showing the world that we are able to meet and conquer you in open war."

Pyrrhus was very much struck with what he considered the extraordinary generosity of his enemies. He immediately collected together all the prisoners that he had taken from the Romans, and sent them home to the Roman camp, as a token of acknowledgment and gratitude on his part for the high and honorable course of action which his adversaries had adopted. They, however, Roman-like, would not accept such a token without making a corresponding return, and they accordingly sent home to Pyrrhus a body of Greek prisoners equal in number and rank to those whom Pyrrhus had set free.

All these things tended to increase the disinclination of Pyrrhus to press the further prosecution of the war. He became more and more desirous every day to make peace with the Romans, preferring very much that such a people should be his allies rather than his enemies. They, however, firmly and pertinaciously refused to treat with him on any terms, unless, as a preliminary step, he would go back to his own dominions. This he thought he could not do with honor. He was accordingly much perplexed, and began earnestly to wish that something would occur to furnish him with a plausible pretext for retiring from Italy.

7

The Sicilian Campaign

B.C. 291-276

Lanassa.—The tyrant her father.—His adventures.—Agathocles's flight from Africa.—Terrible consequences.—The sea dyed with blood.—Shocking story.—Texina and her children.—Extraordinary story.—Mænon's contrivance for administering poison.—Dangers of usurpation.—Mænon's career.—Pyrrhus receives two tempting invitations.—Pyrrhus's perplexity.—He decides to go to Sicily.—He makes great preparations at Tarentum.—The Tarentines remonstrate.—Their arguments.—Pyrrhus sends Cineas in advance to Sicily.—Form of Sicily.—Situation of Messana.—Conduct of the Mamertines in Sicily.—The Mamertines take complete possession of Messana.—Three objects to be accomplished in Sicily.—The grand expedition sails to Sicily.—He determines to take Eryx by storm.—Pyrrhus at the head of the column.—Combat on the walls.—Pyrrhus victorious.—Grand celebration.—Result of the battle.—He attacks the Mamertines.—Is victorious.—Pyrrhus forms new schemes.—Want of seamen.—The Sicilians are opposed to his plans.—General rebellion in Sicily.—Pyrrhus's character.—He possesses no perseverance.—New plan.—Disastrous attempt to get back to Italy.—Terrible conflict.—Pyrrhus is wounded in the head.—Shocking spectacle.—The Mamertine champion.—Pyrrhus succeeds in reaching Tarentum.

THE fact has already been mentioned that one of the wives whom Pyrrhus had married after the death of Antigone, the Egyptian princess, was Lanassa, the daughter of Agathocles, the King of Sicily. Agathocles was a tyrannical monster of the worst description. His army was little better than an organized band of robbers, at the head of which he went forth on marauding and plundering expeditions among all the nations that were within his reach. He made these predatory excursions sometimes into Italy, sometimes into the Carthaginian territories on the African coast, and sometimes among the islands of the Mediterranean Sea. In these campaigns he met with a great variety of adventures, and experienced every possible fate that the fortune of war could bring. Sometimes he was triumphant over all who opposed him, and became intoxicated with prosperity and success. At other times, through his insane and reckless folly, he would involve himself in the most desperate difficulties, and was frequently compelled to give up every thing, and to fly alone in absolute destitution from the field of his attempted exploits to save his life.

On one such occasion, he abandoned an army in Africa, which he had taken there on one of his predatory enterprises, and, flying secretly from the camp, he made his escape with a small number of attendants, leaving the army to its fate. His flight was so sudden on this occasion that he left his two sons behind him in the hands and at the mercy of the soldiers. The soldiers, as soon as they found that Agathocles had gone and left them, were so enraged against him that they put his sons to death on the spot, and then surrendered in a body to the enemy. Agathocles, when the tidings of this transaction came to him in Sicily, was enraged against the soldiers in his turn, and, in order to revenge himself upon them, he immediately sought out from among the population of the country their wives and children, their brothers and sisters, and all who were in any way related to them. These innocent representatives of the absent offenders he ordered to be seized and slain, and their bodies to be cast into the sea toward Africa as an expression of revengeful triumph and defiance. So great was the slaughter on this occasion, that the waters of the sea were dyed with blood to a great distance from the shore.

Of course, such cruelty as this could not be practiced without awakening, on the part of those who suffered from it, a spirit of hatred and revenge. Plots and conspiracies without number were formed against the tyrant's life, and in his later years he lived in continual apprehension and distress. His fate, however, was still more striking as an illustration of the manner in which the old age of ambitious and unprincipled men is often embittered by the ingratitude and wickedness of their children. Agathocles had a grandson named Archagathus, who, if all the accounts are true, brought the old king's gray hairs in sorrow to the grave. The story is too shocking to be fully believed, but it is said that this grandson first murdered Agathocles's son and heir, his own uncle, in order that he might himself succeed to the throne—his own father, who would have been the next heir, being dead. Then, not being willing to wait until the old king himself should die, he began to form plots against his life, and against the lives of the remaining members of the family. Although several of Agathocles's sons were dead, having been destroyed by violence, or having fallen in war, he had a wife, named Texina, and two children still remaining alive. The king was so anxious in respect to these children, on account of Archagathus, that he determined to send them with their mother to Egypt, in order to place them beyond the reach of their merciless nephew. Texina was very unwilling to consent to such a measure. For herself and her sons the proposed retiring into Egypt was little better than going into exile, and she was, moreover, extremely reluctant to leave her husband alone in Syracuse, exposed to the machinations and plots which his unnatural grandson might form against him. She, however, finally submitted to the hard necessity and went away, bidding her husband farewell with many tears. Very soon after her departure her husband died.

The story that is told of the manner of his death is this: There was in his court a man named Mænon, whom Agathocles had taken captive when a youth, and ever since retained in his court. Though originally a captive, taken in war, Mænon had been made a favorite with Agathocles, and had been raised to a high position in his service. The indulgence however, and the favoritism with which he had been regarded, were not such as to awaken any sentiments of gratitude in Mænon's mind, or to establish any true and faithful friendship between him and his master; and Archagathus, the grandson, found means of inducing him to undertake to poison the king. As all the ordinary modes of administering poison were precluded by the vigilance and strictness with which the usual avenues of approach to the king were guarded, Mænon contrived to accomplish his end by poisoning a quill which the king was subsequently to use as a tooth-pick. The poison was insinuated thus into the teeth and gums of the victim, where it soon took effect, producing dreadful ulceration and intolerable pain. The infection of the venom after a short time pervaded the whole system of the sufferer, and brought him to the brink of the grave; and at last, finding that he was speechless, and apparently insensible, his ruthless murderers, fearing, perhaps, that he might revive again, hurried him to the funeral pile before life was extinct, and the fire finished the work that the poison had begun.

The declaration of Scripture, "They that take the sword shall perish by the sword," is illustrated and confirmed by the history of almost every ancient tyrant. We find that they almost all come at last to some terrible end. The man who usurps a throne by violence seems, in all ages and among all nations, very sure to be expelled from it by greater violence, after a brief period of power; and he who poisons or assassinates a precedent rival whom he wishes to supplant, is almost invariably cut off by the poison or the dagger of a following one, who wishes to supplant him.

The death of Agathocles took place about nine years before the campaign of Pyrrhus in Italy, as described in the last chapter, and during that period the kingdom of Sicily had been in a very distracted state. Mænon, immediately after the poisoning of the king, fled to the camp of Archagathus, who was at that time in command of an army at a

THE HISTORY OF PYRRHUS

distance from the city. Here, in a short time, he contrived to assassinate Archagathus, and to seize the supreme power. It was not long, however, before new claimants and competitors for possession of the throne appeared, and new wars broke out, in the course of which Mænon was deposed. At length, in the midst of the contests and commotions that prevailed, two of the leading generals of the Sicilian army conceived the idea of bringing forward Pyrrhus's son by Lanassa as the heir to the crown. This prince was, of course, the grandson of the old King Agathocles, and, as there was no other descendant of the royal line at hand who could be made the representative of the ancient monarchy, it was thought, by the generals above referred to, that the only measure which afforded any hope of restoring peace to the country was to send an embassy to Pyrrhus, and invite him to come and place his young son upon the throne. The name of Lanassa's son was Alexander. He was a boy, perhaps at this time about twelve years old.

At the same time that Pyrrhus received the invitation to go to Sicily, a message came to him from certain parties in Greece, informing him that, on account of some revolutions which had taken place there, a very favorable opportunity was afforded him to secure for himself the throne of that country, and urging him to come and make the attempt. Pyrrhus was for some time quite undecided which of these two proposals to accept. The prize offered him in Greece was more tempting, but the expedition into Sicily seemed to promise more certain success. While revolving the question in his mind which conquest he should first undertake, he complained of the tantalizing cruelty of fortune, in offering him two such tempting prizes at the same time, so as to compel him to forego either the one or the other. At length he decided to go first to Sicily.

It was said that one reason which influenced his mind very strongly in making this decision was the fact that Sicily was so near the coast of Africa; and the Sicilians being involved in wars with the Carthaginians, he thought that, if successful in his operations in Sicily, the way would be open for him to make an expedition into Africa, in which case he did not doubt but that he should be able soon to overturn the Carthaginian power, and add all the northern coasts of Africa to his dominions. His empire would thus embrace Epirus, the whole southern part of Italy, Sicily, and the coasts of Africa. He could afterward, he thought, easily add Greece, and then his dominions would include all the wealthy and populous countries surrounding the most important part of the Mediterranean Sea. His government would thus become a naval power of the first class, and any further extension of his sway which he might subsequently desire could easily be accomplished.

In a word, Pyrrhus decided first to proceed to Sicily, and to postpone for a brief period his designs on Greece.

He accordingly proceeded to withdraw his troops from the interior of the country in Italy, and concentrate them in and around Tarentum. He began to make naval preparations, too, on a very extensive scale. The port of Tarentum soon presented a very busy scene. The work of building and repairing ships—of fabricating sails and rigging—of constructing and arming galleys—of disciplining and training crews—of laying in stores of food and of implements of war, went on with great activity, and engaged universal attention. The Tarentines themselves stood by, while all these preparations were going on, rather as spectators of the scene than as active participants. Pyrrhus had taken the absolute command of their city and government, and was exercising supreme power, as if he were the acknowledged sovereign of the country. He had been invited to come over from his own kingdom to *help* the Tarentines, not to *govern* them; but he had seized the sovereign power, justifying the seizure, as is usual with military men under similar circumstances, by the necessity of the case. "There must be order and submission to authority in the city," he said, "or we can make no progress in subduing our enemies." The Tarentines had thus been induced to submit to his assumption of power, convinced, perhaps, partly by his reasoning, and, at all events, silenced by the display of force by which it was accompanied; and they had consoled themselves under a condition of things which they could not prevent, by considering that it was better to yield to a temporary foreign domination, than to be wholly overwhelmed, as there was every probability, before Pyrrhus came to them, that they would be, by their domestic foes.

When, however, they found that Pyrrhus was intending to withdraw from them, and to go to Sicily, without having really effected their deliverance from the danger which threatened them, they at first remonstrated against the design. They wished him to remain and finish the work which he had begun. The Romans had been checked, but they had not been subdued. Pyrrhus ought not, they said, to go away and leave them until their independence and freedom had been fully established. They remonstrated with him against his design, but their remonstrances proved wholly unavailing.

When at length the Tarentines found that Pyrrhus was determined to go to Sicily, they then desired that he should withdraw his troops from their country altogether, and leave them to themselves. This, however, Pyrrhus refused to do. He had no intention of relinquishing the power which he had acquired in Italy, and he accordingly began to make preparations for leaving a strong garrison in Tarentum to maintain his government there. He organized a sort of regency in the city, and set apart a sufficient force from his army to maintain it in power during his absence. When this was done, he began to make preparations for transporting the rest of his force to Sicily by sea.

He determined to send Cineas forward first, according to his usual custom, to make the preliminary arrangements in Sicily. Cineas consequently left Tarentum with a small squadron of ships and galleys, and, after a short voyage, arrived safely at Syracuse. He found the leading powers in that city ready to welcome Pyrrhus as soon as he should arrive, and make the young Alexander king. Cineas completed and closed the arrangements for this purpose, and then sent messengers to various other cities on the northern side of the island, making known to them the design which had been formed of raising an heir of King Agathocles to the throne, and asking their co-operation in it. He managed these negotiations with so much prudence and skill, that nearly all that part of the island which was in the hands of the Sicilians readily acceded to the plan, and the people were every where prepared to welcome Pyrrhus and the young prince as soon as they should arrive.

Sicily, as will be seen by referring to the map, is of a triangular form. It was only the southern portion which was at this time in the hands of the Sicilians. There were two foreign and hostile powers in possession, respectively, of the northeastern and northwestern portions. In the northeastern corner of the island was the city of Messana—the Messina of modern days. In the time of Pyrrhus's expedition, Messana was the seat and stronghold of a warlike nation, called the Mamertines, who had come over from Italy across the Straits of Messana some years before, and, having made themselves masters of that portion of the island, had since held their ground there, notwithstanding all the efforts of the Sicilians to expel them. The Mamertines had originally come into Sicily, it was said, as Pyrrhus had gone into Italy—by invitation. Agathocles sent for them to come and aid him in some of his wars. After the object for which they had been sent for had been accomplished, Agathocles dismissed his auxiliaries, and they set out on their return. They proceeded through the northeastern part of the island to Messana, where they were to embark for Italy. Though they had rendered Agathocles very efficient aid in his campaigns, they had also occasioned him an infinite deal of trouble by their turbulent and ungovernable spirit; and now, as they were withdrawing from the island, the inhabitants of the country through which they passed on the way regarded them every where with terror and dread. The people of Messana, anxious to avoid a quarrel with them, and disposed to facilitate their peaceable departure from the land by every means in their power, received them into the city, and hospitably entertained them there. Instead, however, of quietly withdrawing from the city in proper time, as the Messanians had expected them to do, they rose suddenly and unexpectedly upon the people, at a concerted signal, took possession of the city, massacred without mercy all the men, seized the women and children, and then, each one establishing himself in the household that choice or chance assigned him, married the wife and adopted the children whose husband and father he had murdered. The result was the most complete and extraordinary overturning that the history of the world can afford. It was a political, a social, and a domestic revolution all in one.

This event took place many years before the time of Pyrrhus's expedition; and though during the interval the Sicilians had made many efforts to dispossess the intruders and to recover possession of Messana, they had not been able to accomplish the work. The Mamertines maintained their ground in Messana, and from that city, as their fortress and stronghold, they extended their power over a considerable portion of the surrounding country.

This territory of the Mamertines was in the northeastern part of the island. In the northwestern part, on the other hand, there was a large province in the hands of the Carthaginians. Their chief city was Eryx; though there was another important city and port, called Lilybæum, which was situated to the southward of Eryx, on the sea-shore. Here the Carthaginians were accustomed to land their re-enforcements and stores; and by means of the ready and direct communication which they could thus keep up with Carthage itself, they were enabled to resist all the efforts which the Sicilians had made to dispossess them.

There were thus three objects to be accomplished by Pyrrhus in Sicily before his dominion over the island could be complete—namely, the Sicilians themselves, in the southern and central parts of the island, were to be conciliated and combined, and induced to give up their intestine quarrels, and to acknowledge the young Alexander as the king of the island; and then the Mamertines on the northeast part, and the Carthaginians in the northwest, were to be conquered and expelled.

The work was done, so far as related to the Sicilians themselves, mainly by Cineas. His dexterous negotiations healed, in a great measure, the quarrels which prevailed among the people, and prepared the way for welcoming Pyrrhus and the young prince, as soon as they should appear. In respect to the Carthaginians and the Mamertines, nothing, of course, could be attempted until the fleets and armies should arrive.

At length the preparations for the sailing of the expedition from Tarentum were completed. The fleet consisted of two hundred sail. The immense squadron, every vessel of which was crowded with armed men, left the harbor of Tarentum, watched by a hundred thousand spectators who had assembled to witness its departure, and slowly made its way along the Italian shores, while its arrival at Syracuse was the object of universal expectation and interest in that city. When at length the fleet appeared in view, entering its port of destination, the whole population of the city and of the surrounding country flocked to the shores to witness the spectacle. Through the efforts which had been made by Cineas, and in consequence of the measures which he had adopted, all ranks and classes of men were ready to welcome Pyrrhus as an expected deliverer. In the name of the young prince, his son, he was to re-establish the ancient monarchy, restore peace and harmony to the land, and expel the hated foreign enemies that infested the confines of it. Accordingly, when the fleet arrived, and Pyrrhus and his troops landed from it, they were received by the whole population with loud and tumultuous acclamations.

After the festivities and rejoicings which were instituted to celebrate Pyrrhus's arrival were concluded, the young Alexander was proclaimed king, and a government was instituted in his name—Pyrrhus himself, of course, being invested with all actual power. Pyrrhus then took the field; and, on mustering his forces, he found himself at the head of thirty or forty thousand men. He first proceeded to attack the Carthaginians. He marched to the part of the island which they held, and gave them battle in the most vigorous and determined manner. They retreated to their cities, and shut themselves up closely within the walls. Pyrrhus advanced to attack them. He determined to carry Eryx, which was the strongest of the Carthaginian cities, by storm, instead of waiting for the slow operations of an ordinary siege. The troops were accordingly ordered to advance at once to the walls, and there mounting, by means of innumerable ladders, to the parapets above, they were to force their way in, over the defenses of the city, in spite of all opposition. Of course, such a service as this is, of all the duties ever required of the soldier, the most dangerous possible. The towers and parapets above, which the assailants undertake to scale, are covered with armed men, who throng to the part of the wall against which the attack is to be directed, and stand there ready with spears, javelins, rocks, and every other conceivable missile, to hurl upon the heads of the besiegers coming up the ladders.

Pyrrhus, however, whatever may have been his faults in other respects, seems to have been very little inclined at any time to order his soldiers to encounter any danger which he was not willing himself to share. He took the head of the column in the storming of Eryx, and was the first to mount the ladders. Previous, however, to advancing for the attack, he performed a grand religious ceremony, in which he implored the assistance of the god Hercules in the encounter which was about to take place; and made a solemn vow that if Hercules would assist him in the conflict, so as to enable him to display before the Sicilians such strength and valor, and to perform such feats as should be worthy of his name, his ancestry, and his past history, he would, immediately after the battle, institute on the spot a course of festivals and sacrifices of the most imposing and magnificent character in honor of the god. This vow being made, the trumpet sounded and the storming party went forward—Pyrrhus at the head of it. In mounting the ladder, he defended himself with his shield from the missiles thrown down upon him from above until he reached the top of the wall, and there, by means of his prodigious strength, and desperate and reckless bravery, he soon gained ground for those that followed him, and established a position there both for himself and for them, having cut down one after another those who attempted to oppose him, until he had surrounded himself with a sort of parapet, formed of the bodies of the dead.

In the mean time, the whole line of ladders extending along the wall were crowded with men, all forcing their way upward against the resistance which the besieged opposed to them from above; while thousands of troops, drawn up below as near as possible to the scene of conflict, were throwing a shower of darts, arrows, javelins, spears, and other missiles, to aid the storming party by driving away the besieged from the top of the wall. By these means those who were mounting the ladders were so much aided in their efforts that they soon succeeded in gaining possession of the wall, and thus made themselves masters of the city.

The Assault

Pyrrhus then, in fulfillment of his vow, instituted a great celebration, and devoted several days to games, spectacles, shows, and public rejoicings of all kinds, intended to express his devout gratitude to Hercules for the divine assistance which the god had vouchsafed to him in the assault by which the city had been carried.

By the result of this battle, and of some other military operations which we can not here particularly describe, the Carthaginians were driven from the open field and compelled to shut themselves up in their strongholds, or retire to the fastnesses of the mountains, where they found places of refuge and defense from which Pyrrhus could not

THE HISTORY OF PYRRHUS

at once dislodge them. Accordingly, leaving things at present as they were in the Carthaginian or western part of the island, he proceeded to attack the Mamertines in the eastern part. He was equally successful here. By means of the tact and skill which he exercised in his military arrangements and maneuvers, and by the desperate bravery and impetuosity which he displayed in battle, he conquered wherever he came. He captured and destroyed many of the strongholds of the Mamertines, drove them entirely out of the open country, and shut them up in Messana. Thus the island was almost wholly restored to the possession of the Sicilians, while yet the foreign intruders, though checked and restrained, were not, after all, really expelled.

The Carthaginians sent messengers to him proposing terms of peace. Their intention was, in these proposals, to retain their province in Sicily, as heretofore, and to agree with Pyrrhus in respect to a boundary, each party being required by the proposed treaty to confine themselves within their respective limits, as thus ascertained. Pyrrhus, however, replied that he could entertain no such proposals. He answered them precisely as the Romans had answered him on a similar occasion, saying that he should insist upon their first retiring from Sicily altogether, as a preliminary step to any negotiations whatever. The Carthaginians would not accede to this demand, and so the negotiations were suspended.

Still the Carthaginians were so securely posted in their strongholds, that Pyrrhus supposed the work of dislodging them by force would be a slow, and tedious, and perhaps doubtful undertaking. His bold and restless spirit accordingly conceived the design of leaving them as they were, and going on in the prosecution of his original design, by organizing a grand expedition for the invasion of Africa. In fact, he thought this would be the most effectual means of getting the Carthaginians out of Sicily; since he anticipated that, if he were to land in Africa, and threaten Carthage itself, the authorities there would be compelled to recall all their forces from foreign lands to defend their own homes and firesides at the capital. He determined, therefore, to equip his fleet for a voyage across the Mediterranean without any delay.

He had ships enough, but he was in want of mariners. In order to supply this want, he began to impress the Sicilians into his service. They were very reluctant to engage in it, partly from natural aversion to so distant and dangerous an enterprise, and partly because they were unwilling that Pyrrhus should leave the island himself until their foreign foes were entirely expelled. "As soon as you have gone," they said, "the Carthaginians and the Mamertines will come out from their hiding-places and retreats, and the country will be immediately involved in all the difficulties from which you have been endeavoring to deliver us. All your labor will have been lost, and we shall sink, perhaps, into a more deplorable condition than ever."

It was evident that these representations were true, but Pyrrhus could not be induced to pay any heed to them. He was determined on carrying into effect his design of a descent upon the coast of Africa. He accordingly pressed forward his preparations in a more arbitrary and reckless spirit than ever. He became austere, imperious, and tyrannical in his measures. He arrested some of the leading generals and ministers of state—men who had been his firmest friends, and through whose agency it was that he had been invited into Sicily, but whom he now suspected of being unfriendly to his designs. One of these men he put to death. In the mean time, he pressed forward his preparations, compelling men to join his army and to embark on board his fleet, and resorting to other harsh and extreme measures, which the people might perhaps have submitted to from one of their own hereditary sovereigns, but which were altogether intolerable when imposed upon them by a foreign adventurer, who had come to their island by their invitation, to accomplish a prescribed and definite duty. In a word, before Pyrrhus was ready to embark on his African campaign, a general rebellion broke out all over Sicily against his authority. Some of the people joined the Mamertines, some the Carthaginians. In a word, the whole country was in an uproar, and Pyrrhus had the mortification of seeing the great

THE HISTORY OF PYRRHUS

fabric of power which, as he imagined, he had been so successfully rearing, come tumbling suddenly on all sides to the ground.

As the reader will have learned long before this time, it was not the nature of Pyrrhus to remain on the spot and grapple with difficulties like these. If there were any new enterprise to be undertaken, or any desperate battle to be fought on a sudden emergency, Pyrrhus was always ready and eager for action, and almost sure of success. But he had no qualities whatever to fit him for the exigencies of such a crisis as this. He had ardor and impetuosity, but no perseverance or decision. He could fight, but he could not plan. He was recklessly and desperately brave in encountering physical danger, but, when involved in difficulties and embarrassments, his only resource was to fly. Accordingly, it was soon announced in Sicily that Pyrrhus had determined to postpone his plan of proceeding to Africa, and was going back to Tarentum, whence he came. He had received intelligence from Tarentum, he said, that required his immediate return to that city. This was probably true; for he had left things in such a condition at Tarentum, that he was, doubtless, continually receiving such intelligence from that quarter. Whether he received any special or extraordinary summons from Tarentum just at this time is extremely uncertain. He, however, pretended that such a message had come; and under this pretense he sheltered himself in his intended departure, so as just to escape the imputation of being actually driven away.

His enemies, however, did not intend to allow him to depart in peace. The Carthaginians, being apprised of his design, sent a fleet to watch the coast and intercept him; while the Mamertines, crossing the Strait, marched to the place on the coast of Italy where they expected he would land, intending to attack him as soon as he should set foot upon the shore. Both these plans were successful. The Carthaginians attacked his fleet, and destroyed many of his ships. Pyrrhus himself barely succeeded in making his escape with a small number of vessels, and reaching the shore. Here, as soon as he gained the land, he was confronted by the Mamertines, who had reached the place before him with ten thousand men. Pyrrhus soon collected from the ships that reached the land a force so formidable that the Mamertines did not dare to attack him in a body, but they blocked up the passes through which the way to Tarentum lay, and endeavored in every way to intercept and harass him in his march. They killed two of his elephants, and cut off many separate detachments of men, and finally deranged all his plans, and threw his whole army into confusion. Pyrrhus at length determined to force his enemies to battle. Accordingly, as soon as a favorable opportunity occurred, he pushed forward at the head of a strong force, and attacked the Mamertines in a sudden and most impetuous manner.

A terrible conflict ensued, in which Pyrrhus, as usual, exposed himself personally in the most desperate manner. In fact, the various disappointments and vexations which he had endured had aroused him to a state of great exasperation against his tormenting enemies. He pushed forward into the hottest part of the battle, his prodigious muscular strength enabling him to beat down and destroy, for a time, all who attempted to oppose him.

At last, however, he received a terrible wound in the head, which, for the moment, entirely disabled him. He was rescued from his peril by his friends, though stunned and fainting under the blow, and was borne off from the scene of conflict with the blood flowing down his face and neck—a frightful spectacle. On being carried to a place of safety within his own ranks, he soon revived, and it was found that he was not dangerously hurt. The enemy, however, full of rage and hatred, came up as near as they dared to the spot where Pyrrhus had been carried, and stood there, calling out to him to come back if he was still alive, and filling the air with taunting and insulting cries, and vociferations of challenge and defiance. Pyrrhus endured this mockery for a few moments as well as he could, but was finally goaded by it into a perfect phrensy of rage. He seized his weapons, pushed his friends and attendants aside, and, in spite of all their remonstrances and all their efforts to restrain him, he rushed forth and assailed his enemies with greater fury than ever. Breathless as he was from his former efforts, and covered with blood and gore, he exhibited a shocking spectacle to all who beheld him. The champion of the Mamertines—the one who had been foremost in challenging Pyrrhus to return—came up to meet him with his weapon upraised. Pyrrhus parried the blow, and then, suddenly bringing down his own sword upon the top of his antagonist's head, he cut the man down, as the story is told, from head to foot, making so complete a division, that one half of the body fell over to one side, and the other half to the other.

It is difficult, perhaps, to assign limits to the degree of physical strength which the human arm is capable of exerting. This fact, however, of cleaving the body of a man by a blow from a sword, was regarded in ancient times as just on the line of absolute impossibility, and was considered, consequently, as the highest personal exploit which a soldier could perform. It was attributed, at different times, to several different warriors, though it is not believed in modern days that the feat was ever really performed.

But, whatever may have been the fate of the Mamertine champion under Pyrrhus's sword, the army itself met with such a discomfiture in the battle that they gave Pyrrhus no further trouble, but, retiring from the field, left him to pursue his march to Tarentum for the remainder of the way in peace. He arrived there at last, with a force in numbers about equal to that with which he had left Tarentum for Sicily. The whole object, however, of his expedition had totally failed. The enterprise, in fact, like almost all the undertakings which Pyrrhus engaged in, though brilliantly and triumphantly successful in the beginning, came only to disappointment and disaster in the end.

8

The Retreat from Italy

B.C. 276-274

State of Pyrrhus's army.—His enfeebled condition.—Precarious situation of his affairs.—Affair of Locri.—Pyrrhus recaptures it.—Proserpina, the Goddess of Death.—Explanations.—Centaurs, mermaids, hippogriffs, and other fables.—Fabulous history of Proserpina.—Ceres seeks her.—Mystical significancy of Proserpina's life.—Pyrrhus resolves to confiscate the treasures at Locri.—The ships are wrecked and the treasures lost.—Pyrrhus is oppressed with superstitious fears.—He goes forth from Tarentum to meet the Romans.—Pyrrhus meets Curius near Beneventum.—He advances through a mountain path by torch-light.—The Romans taken by surprise.—Pyrrhus is repulsed.—Adventures of Pyrrhus on the field of battle.—Onset of the elephants.—They are terrified by the torches.—The young elephant and its mother.—Pyrrhus's flight.—His desperate expedient.—He arrives at length safely in Epirus.

THE force with which Pyrrhus returned to Tarentum was very nearly as large as that which he had taken away, but was composed of very different materials. The Greeks from Epirus, whom he had brought over with him in the first instance from his native land, had gradually disappeared from the ranks of his army. Many of them had been killed in battle, and still greater numbers had been carried off by exposure and fatigue, and by the thousand other casualties incident to such a service as that in which they were engaged. Their places had been supplied, from time to time, by new enlistments, or by impressment and conscription. Of course, these new recruits were not bound to their commander by any ties of attachment or regard. They were mostly mercenaries—that is, men hired to fight, and willing to fight, in any cause or for any commander, provided they could be paid. In a word, Pyrrhus's fellow-countrymen of Epirus had disappeared, and the ranks of his army were filled up with unprincipled and destitute wretches, who felt no interest in his cause—no pride in his success—no concern for his honor. They adhered to him only for the sake of the pay and the indulgences of a soldier's life, and for their occasional hopes of plunder.

Besides the condition of his army, Pyrrhus found the situation of his affairs in other respects very critical on his arrival at Tarentum. The Romans had made great progress, during his absence, in subjugating the whole country to their sway. Cities and towns, which had been under his dominion when he went to Sicily, had been taken by the Romans, or had gone over to them of their own accord. The government which he had established at Tarentum was thus curtailed of power, and shut in in respect to territory; and he felt himself compelled immediately to take the field, in order to recover his lost ground.

He adopted vigorous measures immediately to re-enforce his army, and to obtain the necessary supplies. His treasury was exhausted; in order to replenish it, he dispatched embassadors to his various allies to borrow money. He knew, of course, that a large portion of his army would abandon him immediately so soon as they should find that he was unable to pay them. He was, therefore, quite uneasy for a time in respect to the state of his finances, and he instructed his embassadors to press the urgency of his wants upon his allies in a very earnest manner.

He did not, however, wait for the result of these measures, but immediately commenced active operations in the field. One of his first exploits was the recapture of Locri, a city situated on the southern shore of Italy, as will be seen by the map. This city had been in his possession before he went to Sicily, but it had gone over to the Romans during his absence. Locri was a very considerable town, and the recovery of it from the Romans was considered quite an important gain. The place derived its consequence, in some considerable degree, from a celebrated temple which stood there. It was the temple of Proserpina, the Goddess of Death. This temple was magnificent in its structure, and it was enriched with very costly and valuable treasures. It not only gave distinction to the town in which it stood, but, on account of an extraordinary train of circumstances which occurred in connection with it, it became the occasion of one of the most important incidents in Pyrrhus's history.

Proserpina, as has already been intimated, was the Goddess of Death. It is very difficult for us at the present day to understand and appreciate the conceptions which the Greeks and Romans, in ancient times, entertained of the supernatural beings which they worshiped—those strange creations, in which we see historic truth, poetic fancy, and a sublime superstition so singularly blended. To aid us in rightly understanding this subject, we must remember that in those days the boundaries of what was known as actual reality were very uncertain and vague. Only a very small portion, either of the visible world or of the domain of science and philosophy, had then been explored; and in the thoughts and conceptions of every man, the natural and the true passed by insensible gradations, on every hand, into the monstrous and the supernatural, there being no principles of any kind established in men's minds to mark the boundaries where the true and the possible must end, and all beyond be impossible and absurd. The knowledge, therefore, that men derived from the observation of such truths and such objects as were immediately around them, passed by insensible gradations into the regions of fancy and romance, and all was believed together. They saw lions and elephants in the lands which were near, and which they knew; and they believed in the centaurs, the mermaids, the hippogriffs, and the dragons, which they imagined inhabiting regions more remote. They saw heroes and chieftains in the plains and in the valleys below; and they had no reason to disbelieve in the existence of gods and demi-gods upon the summits of the blue and beautiful mountains above, where, for aught they knew, there might lie boundless territories of verdure and loveliness, wholly inaccessible to man. In the same manner, beneath the earth somewhere, they knew not where, there lay, as they imagined, extended regions destined to receive the spirits of the dead, with approaches leading to it, through mysterious grottoes and caverns, from above. Proserpina was the Goddess of Death, and the queen of these lower abodes.

Various stories were told of her origin and history. The one most characteristic and most minutely detailed is this:

She was the daughter of Jupiter and Ceres. She was very beautiful; and, in order to protect her from the importunity of lovers, her mother sent her, under the care of an attendant named Calligena, to a cavern in Sicily, and concealed her there. The mouth of the cavern was guarded by dragons. Pluto, who was the god of the inferior regions, asked her of Jupiter, her father, for his wife. Jupiter consented, and sent Venus to entice her out of her cavern, that Pluto might obtain her. Venus, attended by Minerva and Diana, proceeded to the cavern where Proserpina was concealed. The three goddesses contrived some means to keep the dragons that guarded the cavern away, and then easily persuaded the maiden to come out to take a walk. Proserpina was charmed with the verdure and beauty which she found around her on the surface of the ground, strongly contrasted as they were with the gloom and desolation of her cavern. She was attended by nymphs and zephyrs in her walk, and in their company she rambled along, admiring the beauty and enjoying the fragrance of the flowers. Some of the flowers which most attracted her attention were produced on the spot by the miraculous power of Jupiter, who caused them to spring up in wonderful luxuriance and splendor, the more effectually to charm the senses of the maiden whom they were enticing away. At length, suddenly the earth opened, and Pluto appeared, coming up from below in a golden chariot drawn by immortal steeds, and, seizing Proserpina, he carried her down to his own abodes.

Ceres, the mother of Proserpina, was greatly distressed when she learned the fate of her daughter. She immediately went to Jupiter, and implored him to restore Proserpina to the upper world. Jupiter, on the other hand, urged Ceres to consent to her remaining as the wife of Pluto. The mother, however, would not yield, and finally her tears and entreaties so far prevailed over Jupiter as to induce him to give permission to Ceres to bring Proserpina back, provided that she had not tasted of any food that grew in the regions below. Ceres accordingly went in search of her daughter. She found, unfortunately, that Proserpina, in walking through the Elysian fields with Pluto, had incautiously eaten a pomegranate which she had taken from a tree that was growing there. She was consequently precluded from availing herself of Jupiter's permission to return to Olympus. Finally, however, Jupiter consented that she should divide her time between the inferior and the superior regions, spending six months with Pluto below, and six months with her mother above; and she did so.

Proserpina was looked upon by all mankind with feelings of great veneration and awe as the goddess and queen of death, and she was worshiped in many places with solemn and imposing ceremonies. There was, moreover, in the minds of men, a certain mystical significancy in the mode of life which she led, in thus dividing her time by regular alternations between the lower and upper worlds, that seemed to them to denote and typify the principle of *vegetation*, which may be regarded as, in a certain sense, alternately a principle of life and death, inasmuch as, for six months in the year, it appears in the form of living and growing plants, rising above the ground, and covering the earth with verdure and beauty, and then, for the six months that remain, it withdraws from the view, and exists only in the form of inert and apparently lifeless roots and seeds, concealed in hidden recesses beneath the ground. Proserpina was thus considered the type and emblem of vegetation, and she was accordingly worshiped, in some sense, as the goddess of resuscitation and life, as well as of death and the grave.

One of the principal temples which had been built in honor of Proserpina was situated, as has already been said, at Locri, and ceremonials and festivals were celebrated here, at stated intervals, with great pomp and parade. This temple had become very wealthy, too, immense treasures having been collected in it, consisting of gold and silver vessels, precious stones, and rich and splendid paraphernalia of every kind—the gifts and offerings which had been made, from time to time, by princes and kings who had attended the festivals.

When Pyrrhus had reconquered Locri from the Romans, and this temple, with all its treasures, fell into his power, some of his advisers suggested that, since he was in such urgent need of money, and all his other plans for supplying himself had hitherto failed, he should take possession of these treasures. They might, it was argued, be considered, in some sense, as public property; and, as the Locrians had revolted from him in his absence, and had now been conquered anew, he was entitled to regard these riches as the spoils of victory. Pyrrhus determined to follow this advice. He took possession of the richest and most valuable of the articles which the temple contained, and, putting them on board ships which he sent to Locri for the purpose, he undertook to transport them to Tarentum. He intended to convert them there into money, in order to obtain funds to supply the wants of his army.

The ships, however, on their passage along the coast, encountered a terrible storm, and were nearly all wrecked and destroyed. The mariners who had navigated the vessels were drowned, while yet the sacred treasures were saved, and that, too, as it would seem, by some supernatural agency, since the same surges which overwhelmed and destroyed the sacrilegious ships and seamen, washed the cases in which the holy treasures had been packed up upon the beach; and there the messengers of Pyrrhus found them, scattered among the rocks and on the sand at various points along the shore. Pyrrhus was greatly terrified at this disaster. He conceived that it was a judgment of Heaven, inflicted upon him through the influence and agency of Proserpina, as a punishment for his impious presumption in despoiling her shrine. He carefully collected all that the sea had saved, and sent every thing back to Locri. He instituted solemn services there in honor of Proserpina, to express his penitence for his faults, and, to give a still more decisive proof of his desire to appease her anger, he put to death the counselors who had advised him to take the treasures.

Notwithstanding all these attempts to atone for his offense, Pyrrhus could not dispel from his mind the gloomy impression which had been made upon it by the idea that he had incurred the direct displeasure of Heaven. He did not believe that the anger of Proserpina was ever fully appeased; and whenever misfortunes and calamities befell him in his subsequent career, he attributed them to the displeasure of the goddess of death, who, as he believed, followed him every where, and was intent on effecting his ruin.

It was now late in the season, and the military operations both of Pyrrhus and of the Romans were, in a great measure, suspended until spring. Pyrrhus spent the interval in making arrangements for taking the field as soon as the winter should be over. He had, however, many difficulties to contend with. His financial embarrassment still continued. His efforts to procure funds were only very partially successful. The people too, in all the region about Tarentum, were, he found, wholly alienated from him. They had not forgiven him for having left them to go to Sicily, and, in consequence of this abandonment of their cause, they had lost much of their confidence in him as their protector, while every thing like enthusiasm in his service was wholly gone. Through these and other causes, he encountered innumerable impediments in executing his plans, and his mind was harassed with continual disappointment and anxiety.

Such, however, was still his resolution and energy, that when the season arrived for taking the field, he had a considerable force in readiness, and he marched out of Tarentum at the head of it, to go and meet the Romans. The Romans themselves, on the other hand, had raised a very large force, and had sent it forward in two divisions, under the command of the two consuls. These two divisions took different routes;

one passing to the north, through the province of Samnium, and the other to the south, through Lucania—both, however, leading toward Tarentum. Pyrrhus divided his forces also into two parts. One body of troops he sent northwardly into Samnium, to meet the northern division of the Roman army, while with the other he advanced himself by the more southern route, to meet the Roman consul who was coming through Lucania. The name of this consul was Curius Dentatus.

Pyrrhus advanced into Lucania. The Roman general, when he found that his enemy was coming, thought it most prudent to send for the other division of his army—namely, the one which was marching through Samnium—and to wait until it should arrive before giving Pyrrhus battle. He accordingly dispatched the necessary orders to Lentulus, who commanded the northern division, and, in the mean time, intrenched himself in a strong encampment at a place called Beneventum. Pyrrhus entered Lucania and advanced toward Beneventum, and, after ascertaining the state of the case in respect to the situation of the camp and the plans of Curius, he paused at some distance from the Roman position, in order to consider what it was best for him to do. He finally came to the conclusion that it was very important that his conflict with the Romans under Curius should take place before Lentulus should arrive to re-enforce them, and so he determined to advance rapidly, and fall upon and surprise them in their intrenchments before they were aware of his approach. This plan he accordingly attempted to execute. He advanced in the ordinary manner and by the public roads of the country until he began to draw near to Beneventum. At the close of the day he encamped as usual; but, instead of waiting in his camp until the following day, and then marching on in his accustomed manner, he procured guides to lead his troops around by a circuitous path among the mountains, with a view of coming down suddenly and unexpectedly upon the camp of the Romans from the hills very early in the morning. An immense number of torches were provided, to furnish light for the soldiers in traversing the dark forests and gloomy ravines through which their pathway lay.

Notwithstanding all the precautions which had been taken, the difficulties of the route were so great that the progress of the troops was very much impeded. The track was every where encumbered with bushes, rocks, fallen trees, and swampy tracts of ground, so that the soldiers made way very slowly. Great numbers of the torches failed in the course of the night, some getting extinguished by accident, and others going out from exhaustion of fuel. By these means great numbers of the troops were left in the dark, and after groping about for a time in devious and uncertain paths, became hopelessly lost in the forest. Notwithstanding all these difficulties and discouragements, however, the main body of the army pressed resolutely on, and, just about daybreak, the van came out upon the heights above the Roman encampment. As soon as a sufficient number were assembled, they were at once marshaled in battle array, and, descending from the mountains, they made a furious onset upon the intrenchments of the enemy.

The Romans were taken wholly by surprise, and their camp became immediately a scene of the wildest confusion. The men started up every where out of their sleep and seized their arms. They were soon in a situation to make a very effectual resistance to the attack of their enemies. They first beat the assailants back from the points where they were endeavoring to gain admission, and then, encouraged by their success, they sallied forth from their intrenchments, and became assailants in their turn. The Greeks were soon overpowered, and forced to retire altogether from the ground. A great many were killed, and some elephants, which Pyrrhus had contrived by some means to bring up to the spot, were taken. The Romans were, of course, greatly elated at this victory.

In fact, so much was Curius gratified and pleased with this success, and so great was the confidence with which it inspired him, that he determined to wait no longer for Lentulus, but to march out at once and give Pyrrhus battle. He accordingly brought forth his troops and drew them up on a plain near his encampment, posting them in such a way as to gain a certain advantage for himself in the nature of the ground which he had chosen, while yet, since there was nothing but the open field between himself and his enemy, the movement was a fair and regular challenge to battle. Pyrrhus accepted this challenge by bringing up his forces to the field, and the conflict began.

As soon as the combatants were fairly engaged, one of the wings of Pyrrhus's army began to give way. The other wing, on the contrary, which was the one that Pyrrhus himself personally commanded, was victorious. Pyrrhus himself led his soldiers on; and he inspired them with so much strength and energy by his own reckless daring, that all those portions of the Roman army which were opposed to them were beaten and driven back into the camp. This success, however, was not wholly owing to the personal prowess of Pyrrhus. It was due, in a great measure, to the power of the elephants, for they fought in that part of the field. As the Romans were almost wholly unaccustomed to the warfare of elephants, they knew not how to resist them, and the huge beasts bore down all before them wherever they moved. In this crisis, Curius ordered a fresh body of troops to advance. It was a corps of reserve, which he had stationed near the camp under orders to hold themselves in readiness there, to come forward and act at any moment, and at any part of the field wherever their services might be required. These troops were now summoned to advance and attack the elephants. They accordingly came rushing on, brandishing their swords in one hand, and bearing burning torches, with which they had been provided for the occasion, in the other. The torches they threw at the elephants as soon as they came near, in order to terrify them and make them unmanageable; and then, with their swords, they attacked the keepers and drivers of the beasts, and the men who fought in connection with them. The success of this onset was so great, that the elephants soon became unmanageable. They even broke into the phalanx, and threw the ranks of it into confusion, overturning and trampling upon the men, and falling themselves upon the slain, under the wounds which the spears inflicted upon them.

The Rout

A remarkable incident is said to have occurred in the midst of this scene of confusion and terror, which strikingly illustrates the strength of the maternal instinct, even among brutes. It happened that there was a young elephant, and also its mother, in the same division of Pyrrhus's army. The former, though young, was sufficiently grown to serve as an elephant of war, and, as it happened, its post on the field of battle was not very far from that of its mother. In the course of the battle the young elephant was wounded, and it uttered immediately a piercing cry of pain and terror. The mother heard the cry, and recognized the voice that uttered it through all the din and uproar of the battle. She immediately became wholly ungovernable, and, breaking away from the control of her keepers, she rushed forward, trampling down every thing in her way, to rescue and protect her offspring. This incident occurred at the commencement of the attack which the Roman reserve made upon the elephants, and contributed very essentially to the panic and confusion which followed.

In the end Pyrrhus was entirely defeated. He was compelled to abandon his camp and to retire toward Tarentum. The Romans immediately advanced, flushed with victory, and carrying all before them. Pyrrhus retreated faster and faster, his numbers continually diminishing as he fled, until at last, when he reached Tarentum, he had only a few horsemen in his train. He sent off the most urgent requests to his friends and allies in Greece to furnish him aid. The help, however, did not come, and Pyrrhus, in order to keep the small remnant that still adhered to him together, resorted to the desperate expedient of forging letters from his friends, promising speedy and abundant supplies, and showing these letters to his officers, to prevent them from being wholly discouraged and abandoning his cause. This miserable contrivance, however, even if successful, could only afford a momentary relief. Pyrrhus soon found that all hope and possibility of retrieving his fortunes in Italy had entirely disappeared, and that no alternative was left to him but to abandon the ground. So, pretending to wonder why his allies did not send forward the succors which they had promised in their letters, and saying that, since they were so dilatory and remiss, he must go himself and bring them, but promising that he would immediately return, he set sail from Tarentum, and, crossing the sea, went home to his own kingdom. He arrived safely in Epirus after an absence of six years.

9

The Family of Lysimachus

B.C. 284-273

Some account of the family of Lysimachus.—Remarks on the principle of hereditary succession.—Difficulties that often occur.—Examples.—Return to the history of Macedon.—Stories of Lysimachus's strength and courage.—Put in a dungeon with a lion.—Amastris and her two sons.—Arsinoe.—Feud in Ptolemy's family.—Origin of the quarrel.—Account of the family.—Ptolemy Ceraunus.—Transfer of the quarrel from Egypt to Macedon.—Lysandra.—Envy and hatred of Arsinoe.—Lysandra's husband imprisoned.—Danger of her children.—Lysandra's flight.—An army raised.—Desperate battle.—Ptolemy Ceraunus.—His reckless and desperate character.—Alliance of Ceraunus with Seleucus.—His plans.—Ceraunus's meditated treachery.—Argos.—Ceraunus proceeds to Macedon.—His rivals and enemies.—Their various claims.—The first contest was with Antigonus.—Arsinoe and her children.—Their retreat to Cassandria.—Ceraunus proposes marriage to Arsinoe.—Ceraunus finds himself in great prosperity.—Invasion threatened.—Ceraunus prepares to defend himself.—Ceraunus thrown to the ground and killed.—Consequences of the death of Ceraunus.

THE reader will perhaps recollect that when Pyrrhus withdrew from Macedon, before he embarked on his celebrated expedition into Italy, the enemy before he was compelled to retire was Lysimachus. Lysimachus continued to reign in Macedon for some time after Pyrrhus had gone, until, finally, he was himself overthrown, under circumstances of a very remarkable character. In fact, his whole history affords a striking illustration of the nature of the results which often followed, in ancient times, from the system of government which then almost universally prevailed—a system in which the supreme power was considered as rightfully belonging to some sovereign who derived it from his ancestors by hereditary descent, and who, in the exercise of it, was entirely above all sense of responsibility to the subjects of his dominion.

It has sometimes been said by writers on the theory of civil government that the principle of hereditary sovereignty in the government of a nation has a decided advantage over any elective mode of designating the chief magistrate, on account of its *certainty*. If the system is such that, on the death of a monarch, the supreme power descends to his eldest son, the succession is determined at once, without debate or delay. If, on the other hand, an election is to take place, there must be a contest. Parties are formed; plans and counterplans are laid; a protracted and heated controversy ensues; and when, finally, the voting is ended, there is sometimes doubt and uncertainty in ascertaining the true result, and very often an angry and obstinate refusal to acquiesce in it when it is determined. Thus the principle of hereditary descent seems simple, clear, and liable to no uncertainty or doubt, while that of popular election tends to lead the country subject to it into endless disputes, and often ultimately to civil war.

But though this may be in *theory* the operation of the two systems, in actual practice it has been found that the hereditary principle has very little advantage over any other in respect to the avoidance of uncertainty and dispute. Among the innumerable forms and phases which the principle of hereditary descent assumes in actual life, the cases in which one acknowledged and unquestioned sovereign of a country dies, and leaves one acknowledged and unquestioned heir, are comparatively few. The relationships existing among the various branches of a family are often extremely intricate and complicated. Sometimes they become variously entangled with each other by intermarriages; sometimes the claims arising under them are disturbed, or modified, or confused by conquests and revolutions; and thus they often become so hopelessly involved that no human sagacity can classify or arrange them. The case of France at the present time is a striking illustration of this difficulty, there being in that country no less than three sets of claimants who regard themselves entitled to the supreme power—the representatives, namely, of the Bourbon, the Orleans, and the Napoleon dynasties. Each one of the great parties rests the claim which they severally advance in behalf of their respective candidates more or less exclusively on rights derived from their hereditary relationship to former rulers of the kingdom, and there is no possible mode of settling the question between them but by the test of power. Even if all concerned were disposed to determine the controversy by a peaceful appeal to the principles of the law of descent, as relating to the transmission of governmental power, no principles could be found that would apply to the case; or, rather, so numerous are the principles that would be required to be taken into the account, and so involved and complicated are the facts to which they must be applied, that any distinct solution of the question on theoretical grounds would be utterly impossible. There is, and there can be, no means of solving such a question but power.

In fact, the history of the smaller monarchies of ancient times is comprised, sometimes for centuries almost exclusively, in narratives of the intrigues, the contentions, and the bloody wars of rival families, and rival branches of the same family, in asserting their respective claims as inheritors to the possession of power. This truth is strikingly illustrated in the events which occurred in Macedon during the absence of Pyrrhus in Italy and Sicily, in connection with the family of Lysimachus, and his successor in power there. These events we shall now proceed to relate in their order.

At the time when Pyrrhus was driven from Macedon by Lysimachus, previous to his going into Italy, Lysimachus was far advanced in age.

THE HISTORY OF PYRRHUS

He was, in fact, at this time nearly seventy years old. He commenced his military career during the lifetime of Alexander the Great, having been one of the great conqueror's most distinguished generals. Many stories were told, in his early life, of his personal strength and valor. On one occasion, as was said, when hunting in Syria, he encountered a lion of immense size single-handed, and, after a very desperate and obstinate conflict, he succeeded in killing him, though not without receiving severe wounds himself in the contest. Another story was, that at one time, having displeased Alexander, he was condemned to suffer death, and that, too, in a very cruel and horrible manner. He was to be thrown into a lion's den. This was a mode of execution not uncommon in ancient times. It answered a double purpose; it not only served for a terrible punishment in respect to the man, but it also effected a useful end in respect to the animal. By giving him a living man to seize and devour, the savage ferocity of the beast was stimulated and increased, and thus he was rendered more valuable for the purposes and uses for which he was retained. In the case of Lysimachus, however, both these objects failed. As soon as he was put into the dungeon where the lion was awaiting him, he attacked the beast, and, though unarmed, he succeeded in destroying him. Alexander admired so much the desperate strength and courage evinced by this exploit, that he pardoned the criminal and restored him to favor.

Lysimachus continued in the service of Alexander as long as that monarch lived; and when, at the death of Alexander, the empire was divided among the leading generals, the kingdom of Thrace, which adjoins Macedon on the east, was assigned to him as his portion. He is commonly designated, therefore, in history, as the King of Thrace; though in the subsequent part of his life he obtained possession also, by conquest, of the kingdom of Macedon. He married, in succession, several wives, and experienced through them a great variety of domestic troubles. His second wife was a Sicilian princess named Amastris. She was a widow at the time of her marriage with Lysimachus, and had two sons. After being married to her for some time, Lysimachus repudiated and abandoned her, and she returned to Sicily with her two sons, and lived in a certain city which belonged to them there. The young men were not of age, and Amastris accordingly assumed the government of the city in their name. They, however, quarreled with their mother, and finally drowned her, in order to remove her out of their way. Lysimachus, though he might justly have considered himself as in some sense the cause of this catastrophe, since, by deserting his wife and withdrawing his protection from her, he compelled her to return to Sicily and put herself in the power of her unnatural sons, was still very indignant at the event, and, fitting out an expedition, he went to Sicily, captured the city, took the sons of Amastris prisoners, and put them to death without mercy, in retribution for their atrocious crime.

At the time when Lysimachus put away his wife, Amastris, he married Arsinoe, an Egyptian princess, the daughter, in fact, of Ptolemy, the son of Lagus, who was at this time the king of Egypt. How far Lysimachus was governed, in his repudiation of Amastris, by the influence of Arsinoe's personal attractions in winning his heart away from his fidelity to his legitimate wife, and how far, on the other hand, he was alienated from her by her own misconduct or the violence of her temper, is not now known. At any rate, the Sicilian wife, as has been stated, was dismissed and sent home, and the Egyptian princess came into her place.

The small degree of domestic peace and comfort which Lysimachus had hitherto enjoyed was far from being improved by this change. The family of Ptolemy was distracted by a deadly feud, and, by means of the marriage of Arsinoe with Lysimachus, and of another marriage which subsequently occurred, and which will be spoken of presently, the quarrel was transferred, in all its bitterness, to the family of Lysimachus, where it produced the most dreadful results.

The origin of the quarrel in the household of Ptolemy was this: Ptolemy married, for his first wife, Eurydice, the daughter of Antipater. When Eurydice, at the time of her marriage, went with her husband into Egypt, she was accompanied by her cousin Berenice, a young and beautiful widow, whom she invited to go with her as her companion and friend. A great change, however, soon took place in the relations which they sustained to each other. From being very affectionate and confidential friends, they became, as often happens in similar cases, on far less conspicuous theatres of action, rivals and enemies. Berenice gained the affections of Ptolemy, and at length he married her. Arsinoe, whom Lysimachus married, was the daughter of Ptolemy and Berenice. They had also a son who was named Ptolemy, and who, at the death of his father, succeeded him on the throne. This son subsequently became renowned in history under the name of Ptolemy Philadelphus. He was the second monarch of the Ptolemaic line.

But, besides these descendants of Berenice, there was another set of children in Ptolemy's family—namely, those by Eurydice. Eurydice had a son and a daughter. The name of the son was Ptolemy Ceraunus; that of the daughter was Lysandra. There was, of course, a standing and bitter feud always raging between these two branches of the royal household. The two wives, though they had once been friends, now, of course, hated each other with perfect hatred. Each had her own circle of partisans and adherents, and the court was distracted for many years with the intrigues, the plots, the dissensions, and the endless schemes and counterschemes which were resorted to by the two parties in their efforts to thwart and circumvent each other. As Arsinoe, the wife of Lysimachus, was the daughter of Berenice, it might have been expected that the influence of Berenice's party would prevail in Lysimachus's court. This would doubtless have been the case, had it not been that unfortunately there was another alliance formed between the two families which complicated the connection, and led, in the end, to the most deplorable results. This other alliance was the marriage of Agathocles, the son of Lysimachus, with Lysandra, Eurydice's daughter. Thus, in the court and family of Lysimachus, Berenice had a representative in the person of her daughter Arsinoe, the wife of the king himself; while Eurydice, also, had one in the person of her daughter Lysandra, the wife of the king's son. Of course, the whole virulence of the quarrel was spread from Egypt to Macedon, and the household of Lysimachus was distracted by the dissensions of Arsinoe and Lysandra, and by the attempts which each made to effect the destruction of the other.

Of course, in this contest, the advantage was on the side of Arsinoe, since she was the wife of the king himself, while Lysandra was only the wife of his son. Still, the position and the influence of Lysandra were very high. Agathocles was a prince of great consideration and honor. He had been very successful in his military campaigns, had won many battles, and had greatly extended the dominion and power of his father. He was a great favorite, in fact, both with the army and with the people, all of whom looked up to him as the hope and the pride of the kingdom.

Of course, the bestowal of all this fame and honor upon Lysandra's husband only served to excite the rivalry and hatred of Arsinoe the more. She and Lysandra were sisters, or, rather, half-sisters—being daughters of the same father. They were, however, on this very account, natural enemies to each other, for their mothers were rivals. Arsinoe, of course, was continually devising means to curtail the growing importance and greatness of Agathocles. Agathocles himself, on the other hand, would naturally make every effort to thwart and counteract her designs. In the end, Arsinoe succeeded in convincing Lysimachus that Agathocles was plotting a conspiracy against him, and was intending to take the kingdom into his own hands. This may have been true. Whether it was true or false, however, can now never be known. At all events, Lysimachus was induced to believe it. He ordered Agathocles to be seized and put into prison, and then, a short time afterward, he caused him to be poisoned. Lysandra was overwhelmed with consternation and sorrow at this event. She was, moreover, greatly alarmed for herself and for her children, and also for her brother, Ptolemy Ceraunus, who was with her at this time. It was obvious that there could be no longer any safety for her in Macedon, and so, taking with her her children, her brother, and a few friends who adhered to her cause, she made her escape from Macedon and went to Asia. Here she cast herself upon the protection of Seleucus, king of Syria.

Seleucus was another of the generals of Alexander—the only one, in fact, besides Lysimachus, who now survived. He had, of course, like Lysimachus, attained to a very advanced period of life, being at this time more than seventy-five years old. These veterans might have been supposed to have lived long enough to have laid aside their ancient rivalries, and to have been willing to spend their few remaining years in peace. But it was far otherwise in fact. Seleucus was pleased with the pretext afforded him, by the coming of Lysandra, for embarking in new wars. Lysandra was, in a short time, followed in her flight by many of the nobles and chieftains of Macedon, who had espoused her cause. Lysimachus, in fact, had driven them away by the severe measures which he had adopted against them. These men assembled at the court of Seleucus, and there, with Lysander and Ptolemy Ceraunus, they began to form plans for invading the dominions of Lysimachus, and avenging the cruel death of Agathocles. Seleucus was very easily induced to enter into these plans, and war was declared.

Lysimachus did not wait for his enemies to invade his dominions; he organized an army, crossed the Hellespont, and marched to meet Seleucus in Asia Minor. The armies met in Phrygia. A desperate battle was fought. Lysimachus was conquered and slain.

Seleucus now determined to cross the Hellespont himself, and, advancing into Thrace and Macedon, to annex those kingdoms to his own domains. Ptolemy Ceraunus accompanied him. This Ptolemy, it will be recollected, was the son of Ptolemy, king of Egypt, by his wife Eurydice; and, at first view, it might seem that he could have no claim whatever himself to the crown of Macedon. But Eurydice, his mother, was the daughter of Antipater, the general to whom Macedon had been assigned on the original division of the empire after Alexander's death. Antipater had reigned over the kingdom for a long time with great splendor and renown, and his name and memory were still held in great veneration by all the Macedonians. Ptolemy Ceraunus began to conceive, therefore, that he was entitled to succeed to the kingdom as the grandson and heir of the monarch who was Alexander's immediate successor, and whose claims were consequently, as he contended, entitled to take precedence of all others.

Moreover, Ptolemy Ceraunus had lived for a long time in Macedon, at the court of Lysimachus, having fled there from Egypt on account of the quarrels in which he was involved in his father's family. He was a man of a very reckless and desperate character, and, while a young man in his father's court, he had shown himself very ill able to brook the preference which his father was disposed to accord to Berenice and to her children over his mother Eurydice and him. In fact, it was said that one reason which led his father to give Berenice's family the precedence over that of Eurydice, and to propose that *her* son rather than Ptolemy Ceraunus should succeed him, was the violent and uncontrollable spirit which Ceraunus displayed. At any rate, Ceraunus quarreled openly with his father, and went to Macedon to join his sister there. He had subsequently spent some considerable time at the court of Lysimachus, and had taken some active part in public affairs. When Agathocles was poisoned, he fled with Lysandra to Seleucus; and when the preparations were made by Seleucus for war with Lysimachus, he probably regarded himself as in some sense the leader of the expedition. He considered Seleucus as his ally, going with him to aid him in the attempt to recover the kingdom of his ancestors.

Seleucus, however, had no such design. He by no means considered himself as engaged in prosecuting an expedition for the benefit of Ceraunus. *His* plan was the enlargement of his own dominion; and as for Ceraunus, he regarded him only as an adventurer following in his train—a useful auxiliary, perhaps, but by no means entitled to be considered as a principal in the momentous transactions which were taking place. Ceraunus, when he found what the state of the case really was, being wholly unscrupulous in respect to the means that he employed for the attainment of his ends, determined to kill Seleucus on the first opportunity.

Seleucus seems to have had no suspicion of this design, for he advanced into Thrace, on his way to Macedon, without fear, and without taking any precautions to guard himself from the danger of Ceraunus's meditated treachery. At length he arrived at a certain town which they told him was called Argos. He seemed alarmed on hearing this name, and, when they inquired the reason, he said that he had been warned by an oracle, at some former period of his life, to beware of Argos, as a place that was destined to be for him the scene of some mysterious and dreadful danger. He had supposed that another Argos was alluded to in this warning, namely, an Argos in Greece. He had not known before of the existence of any Argos in Thrace. If he had been aware of it, he would have ordered his march so as to have avoided it altogether; and now, in consequence of the anxious forebodings that were excited by the name, he determined to withdraw from the place without delay. He was, however, overtaken by his fate before he could effect his resolution. Ptolemy Ceraunus, watching a favorable opportunity which occurred while he was at Argos, came stealthily up behind the aged king, and stabbed him in the back with a dagger. Seleucus immediately fell down and died.

Ptolemy Ceraunus forthwith organized a body of adherents and proceeded to Macedon, where he assumed the diadem, and caused himself to be proclaimed king. He found the country distracted by dissensions, many parties having been formed, from time to time, in the course of the preceding reigns, each of which was now disposed to come forward with its candidates and its claims. All these Ptolemy Ceraunus boldly set aside. He endeavored to secure all those who were friendly to the ancient house of Antipater by saying that he was Antipater's grandson and heir; and, on the other hand, to conciliate the partisans of Lysimachus, by saying that he was Lysimachus's avenger. This was in one sense true, for he had murdered Seleucus, the man by whom Lysimachus had been destroyed. He relied, however, after all, for the means of sustaining himself in his new position, not on his reasons, but on his troops; and he accordingly advanced into the country more as a conqueror coming to subjugate a nation by force, than as a prince succeeding peacefully to an hereditary crown.

He soon had many rivals and enemies in the field against him. The three principal ones were Antiochus, Antigonus, and Pyrrhus. Antiochus was the son of Seleucus. He maintained that his father had fairly conquered the kingdom of Macedon, and had acquired the right to reign over it; that Ptolemy Ceraunus, by assassinating Seleucus, had not divested him of any of his rights, but that they all descended unimpaired to his son, and that he himself, therefore, was the true king of Macedon. Antigonus was the son of Demetrius, who had reigned in Macedon at a former period, before Lysimachus had invaded and conquered the kingdom. Antigonus therefore maintained that his right was superior to that of Ptolemy, for his father had been the acknowledged sovereign of the country at a period subsequent to that of the reign of Antipater. Pyrrhus was the third claimant. He had held Macedon by conquest immediately before the reign of Lysimachus, and now, since Lysimachus had been deposed, his rights, as he alleged, revived. In a word, there were four competitors for the throne, each urging claims compounded of rights of conquest and of inheritance, so complicated and so involved, one with the other, as to render all attempts at a peaceable adjudication of them absolutely hopeless. There could be no possible way of determining who was best entitled to the throne in such a case. The only question, therefore, that remained was, who was best able to take and keep it.

This question Ptolemy Ceraunus had first to try with Antigonus, who came to invade the country with a fleet and an army from Greece. After a very short but violent contest, Antigonus was defeated, both by sea and by land, and Ceraunus remained master of the kingdom. This triumph greatly strengthened his power in respect to the other competitors. He, in fact, contrived to settle the question with them by treaty, in which they acknowledged him as king. In the case of Pyrrhus, he agreed, in consideration of being allowed peaceably to retain possession of his kingdom, to furnish a certain amount of military aid to strengthen the hands of Pyrrhus in the wars in which he was then engaged in Italy and

Sicily. The force which he thus furnished consisted of five thousand foot, four thousand horse, and fifty elephants.

Thus it would seem that every thing was settled. There was, however, one difficulty still remaining. Arsinoe, the widow of Lysimachus, still lived. It was Arsinoe, it will be recollected, whose jealousy of her half-sister, Lysandra, had caused the death of Agathocles and the flight of Lysandra, and which had led to the expedition of Seleucus, and the subsequent revolution in Macedon. When her husband was killed, she, instead of submitting at once to the change of government, shut herself up in Cassandria, a rich and well-defended city. She had her sons with her, who, as the children of Lysimachus, were heirs to the throne. She was well aware that she had, for the time being, no means at her command for supporting the claims of her children, but she was fully determined not to relinquish them, but to defend herself and her children in the city of Cassandria, as well as she was able, until some change should take place in the aspect of public affairs. Ceraunus, of course, saw in her a very formidable and dangerous opponent; and, after having triumphed over Antigonus, and concluded his peace with Antiochus and with Pyrrhus, he advanced toward Cassandria, revolving in his mind the question by what means he could best manage to get Arsinoe and her children into his power.

He concluded to try the effect of cunning and treachery before resorting to force. He accordingly sent a message to Arsinoe, proposing that, instead of quarreling for the kingdom, they should unite their claims, and asking her, for this purpose, to become his wife. He would marry her, he said, and adopt her children as his own, and thus the whole question would be amicably settled.

Arsinoe very readily acceded to this proposal. It is true that she was the half-sister of Ceraunus; but this relationship was no bar to a matrimonial union, according to the ideas that prevailed in the courts of kings in those days. Arsinoe, accordingly, gave her consent to the proposal, and opened the gates of the city to Ceraunus and his troops. Ceraunus immediately put her two sons to death. Arsinoe herself fled from the city. Very probably Ceraunus allowed her to escape, since, as she herself had no claim to the throne, any open violence offered to her would have been a gratuitous crime, which would have increased, unnecessarily, the odium that would naturally attach to Ceraunus's proceedings. At any rate, Arsinoe escaped, and, after various wanderings, found her way back to her former home in her father's court at Alexandria.

The heart of Ceraunus was now filled with exultation and pride. All his schemes had proved successful, and he found himself, at last, in secure possession, as he thought, of a powerful and wealthy kingdom. He wrote home to his brother in Egypt, Ptolemy Philadelphus— by whom, as the reader will recollect, he had been supplanted there, in consequence of his father's preference for the children of Berenice— saying that he now acquiesced in that disposition of the kingdom of Egypt, since he had acquired for himself a better kingdom in Macedon. He proceeded to complete the organization of his government. He recruited his armies; he fortified his towns; and began to consider himself as firmly established on his throne. All his dreams, however, of security and peace, were soon brought to a very sudden termination.

There was a race of half-civilized people on the banks of the Danube called Gauls. Some tribes of this nation afterward settled in what is now France, and gave their name to that country. At the period, however, of the events which we are here relating, the chief seat of their dominion was a region on the banks of the Danube, north of Macedon and Thrace. Here they had been for some time concentrating their forces and gradually increasing in power, although their movements had been very little regarded by Ceraunus. Now, however, a deputation suddenly appeared at Ceraunus's capital, to say that they were prepared for an invasion of his dominions, and asking him how much money he would give for peace. Ceraunus, in the pride of his newly-established power, treated this proposal with derision. He directed the embassadors to go back and say that, far from wishing to purchase peace, he would not *allow* peace to them, unless they immediately sent him all their principal generals, as hostages for their good behavior. Of course, after such an interchange of messages as this, both parties immediately prepared for war.

Ceraunus assembled all the forces that he could command, marched northward to meet his enemy, and a great battle was fought between the two armies. Ceraunus commanded in person in this conflict. He rode into the field at the head of his troops, mounted on an elephant. In the course of the action he was wounded, and the elephant on which he rode becoming infuriated at the same time, perhaps from being wounded himself too, threw his rider to the ground. The Gauls who were fighting around him immediately seized him. Without any hesitation or delay they cut off his head, and, raising it on the point of a pike, they bore it about the field in triumph. This spectacle so appalled and intimidated the army of the Macedonians, that the ranks were soon broken, and the troops, giving way, fled in all directions, and the Gauls found themselves masters of the field.

The Fallen Elephant

The death of Ptolemy Ceraunus was, of course, the signal for all the old claimants to the throne to come forward with their several pretensions anew. A protracted period of dissension and misrule ensued, during which the Gauls made dreadful havoc in all the northern portions of Macedon. Antigonus at last succeeded in gaining the advantage, and obtained a sort of nominal possession of the throne, which he held until the time when Pyrrhus returned to Epirus from Italy. Pyrrhus, being informed of this state of things, could not resist the desire which he felt of making an incursion into Macedon, and seizing for himself the prize for which rivals, no better entitled to it than he, were so fiercely contending.

10

The Reconquest of Macedon

B.C. 273-272

Fatal deficiencies in Pyrrhus's character.—Fickleness of Pyrrhus.—Consequences which resulted from it.—Examples of his want of perseverance.—Reasons for the proposed invasion of Macedon.—In the outset Pyrrhus is successful.—The country is disposed to submit to him.—Combat in the mountain defile.—Account of the phalanx.—Its terrible efficacy.—Impossibility of making any impression upon it.—The elephants.—Order of battle.—The elephants overpowered.—The phalanx.—Pyrrhus invites the enemy to join him.—Pyrrhus is victorious, and becomes master of Macedon.—Complaints of the people.—Pyrrhus pays little regard to them.—Pyrrhus receives an unexpected invitation.

IT was the great misfortune of Pyrrhus's life, a misfortune resulting apparently from an inherent and radical defect in his character, that he had no settled plans or purposes, but embarked in one project after another, as accident or caprice might incline him, apparently without any forethought, consideration, or design. He seemed to form no plan, to live for no object, to contemplate no end, but was governed by a sort of blind and instinctive impulse, which led him to love danger, and to take a wild and savage delight in the performance of military exploits on their own account, and without regard to any ultimate end or aim to be accomplished by them. Thus, although he evinced great power, he produced no permanent effects. There was no steadiness or perseverance in his action, and there could be none, for in his whole course of policy there were no ulterior ends in view by which perseverance could be sustained. He was, consequently, always ready to abandon any enterprise in which he might be engaged as soon as it began to be involved in difficulties requiring the exercise of patience, endurance, and self-denial, and to embark in any new undertaking, provided that it promised to bring him speedily upon a field of battle. He was, in a word, the type and exemplar of that large class of able men who waste their lives in a succession of efforts, which, though they evince great talent in those who perform them, being still without plan or aim, end without producing any result. Such men often, like Pyrrhus, attain to a certain species of greatness. They are famed among men for what they seem to have the power to do, and not for any thing that they have actually done.

In accordance with this view of Pyrrhus's character, we see him changing continually the sphere of his action from one country to another, gaining great victories every where, and evincing in all his operations—in the organizing and assembling of his armies, in his marches, in his encampments, and in the disposition of his troops on the field of battle, and especially in his conduct during the period of actual conflict—the most indomitable energy and the most consummate military skill. But when the battle was fought and the victory gained, and an occasion supervened requiring a cool and calculating deliberation in the forming of future plans, and a steady adherence to them when formed, the character and resources of Pyrrhus's mind were found woefully wanting. The first summons from any other quarter, inviting him to a field of more immediate excitement and action, was always sufficient to call him away. Thus he changed his field of action successively from Macedon to Italy, from Italy to Sicily, from Sicily back to Italy, and from Italy to Macedon again, perpetually making new beginnings, but nowhere attaining any ends.

His determination to invade Macedon once more, on his return to Epirus from Italy, was prompted, apparently, by the mere accident that the government was unsettled, and that Antigonus was insecure in his possession of the throne. He had no intention, when he first embarked in this scheme, of attempting the conquest of Macedon, but only designed to make a predatory incursion into the country for the purpose of plunder, its defenseless condition affording him, as he thought, a favorable opportunity of doing this. The plea on which he justified this invasion was, that Antigonus was his enemy. Ptolemy Ceraunus had made a treaty of alliance with him, and had furnished him with troops for recruiting and re-enforcing his armies in Italy, as has already been stated; but Antigonus, when called upon, had refused to do this. This, of course, gave Pyrrhus ample justification, as he imagined, for his intended incursion into the Macedonian realms.

Besides this, however, there was another justification, namely, that of necessity. Although Pyrrhus had been compelled to withdraw from Italy, he had not returned by any means alone, but had brought quite a large army with him, consisting of many thousands of men, all of whom must now be fed and paid. All the resources of his own kingdom had been wellnigh exhausted by the drafts which he had made upon them to sustain himself in Italy, and it was now necessary, he thought, to embark in some war, as a means of finding employment and subsistence for these troops. He determined, therefore, on every account, to make a foray into Macedon.

Before setting off on his expedition, he contrived to obtain a considerable force from among the Gauls as auxiliaries. Antigonus, also, had Gauls in his service, for they themselves were divided, as it would seem, in respect both to their policy and their leaders, as well as the Macedonians; and Antigonus, taking advantage of their dissensions, had contrived to enlist some portion of them in his cause, while the rest were the more easily, on that very account, induced to join the expedition of Pyrrhus. Things being in this state, Pyrrhus, after completing his preparations, commenced his march, and soon crossed the Macedonian frontier.

As was usually the case with the enterprises which he engaged in, he was, in the outset, very successful. He conquered several cities and towns as he advanced, and soon began to entertain higher views in respect to the object of his expedition than he had at first formed. Instead of merely plundering the frontier, as he had at first intended, he began to think that it would be possible for him to subdue Antigonus entirely, and reannex the whole of Macedon to his dominions. He was well known in Macedon, his former campaigns in that country having brought him very extensively before the people and the army there. He had been a general favorite, too, among them at the time when he had been their ruler; the people admired his personal qualities as a soldier, and had been accustomed to compare him with Alexander, whom, in his appearance and manners, and in a certain air of military frankness and generosity which characterized him, he was said strongly to resemble. Pyrrhus now found, as he advanced into the country of Macedonia, that the people were disposed to regard him with the same sentiments of favor which they had formerly entertained for him. Several of the garrisons of the cities joined his standard; and the detachments of troops which Antigonus sent forward to the frontier to check his progress, instead of giving him battle, went over to him in a body and espoused his cause. In a word, Pyrrhus found that, unexpectedly to himself, his expedition, instead of being merely an incursion across the frontiers on a plundering foray, was assuming the character of a regular invasion. In short, the progress that he made was such, that it soon became manifest that to meet Antigonus in one pitched battle, and to gain one victory, was all that was required to complete the conquest of the country.

He accordingly concentrated his forces more and more, strengthened himself by every means in his power, and advanced further and further into the interior of the country. Antigonus began to retire, desirous, perhaps, of reaching some ground where he could post himself advantageously. Pyrrhus, acting with his customary energy, soon overtook the enemy. He came up with the rear of Antigonus's army in a narrow defile among the mountains; at least, the place is designated as a narrow defile by the ancient historian who narrates these events, though, from the number of men that were engaged in the action which ensued, as well as from the nature of the action itself, as a historian describes it, it would seem that there must have been a considerable breadth of level ground in the bottom of the gorge.

The main body of Antigonus's troops was the phalanx. The Macedonian phalanx is considered one of the most extraordinary military contrivances of ancient times. The invention of it was ascribed to Philip, the father of Alexander the Great, though it is probable that it was only improved and perfected, and brought into general use, but not really originated by him. The single phalanx was formed of a body of about four thousand men. These men were arranged in a compact form, the whole body consisting of sixteen ranks, and each rank of two hundred and fifty-six men. These men wore each a short sword, to be used in cases of emergency, and were defended by large shields. The main peculiarity, however, of their armor, and the one on which the principal power of the phalanx depended as a military body, was in the immensely long spears which they carried. These spears were generally twenty-one, and sometimes twenty-four feet long. The handles were slender, though strong, and the points were tipped with steel. The spears were not intended to be thrown, but to be held firmly in the hands, and pointed toward the enemy; and they were so long, and the ranks of the men were so close together, that the spears of the fifth rank projected several feet before the men who stood in the front rank. Thus each man in the front rank had five steel-pointed spears projecting to different distances before him, while the men who stood in ranks further behind rested their spears upon the shoulders of those who were before them, so as to elevate the points into the air.

The men were protected by large shields, which, when the phalanx was formed in close array, just touched each other, and formed an impregnable defense. In a word, the phalanx, as it moved slowly over the plain, presented the appearance of a vast monster, covered with scales, and bristling with points of steel—a sort of military porcupine, which nothing could approach or in any way injure. Missiles thrown toward it were intercepted by the shields, and fell harmless to the ground. Darts, arrows, javelins, and every other weapon which could be projected from a distance, were equally ineffectual, and no one could come near enough to men thus protected to strike at them with the sword. Even cavalry were utterly powerless in attacking such *chevaux de frise* as the phalanx presented. No charge, however furious, could break its serrated ranks; an onset upon it could only end in impaling the men and the horses that made it together on the points of the innumerable spears.

To form a phalanx, and to maneuver it successfully, required a special training, both on the part of the officers and men, and in the Macedonian armies the system was carried to very high perfection. When foreign auxiliaries, however, served under Macedonian generals, they were not generally formed in this way, but were allowed to fight under their own leaders, and in the accustomed manner of their respective nations. The army of Antigonus, accordingly, as he was retiring before Pyrrhus, consisted of two portions. The phalanx was in advance, and large bodies of Gauls, armed and arrayed in their usual manner, were in the rear. Of course, Pyrrhus, as he came up with this force in the ravine or valley, encountered the Gauls first. Their lines, it would seem, filled up the whole valley at the place where Pyrrhus overtook them, so that, at the outset of the contest, Pyrrhus had them only to engage. There was not space sufficient for the phalanx to come to their aid.

Besides the phalanx and the bodies of Gauls, there was a troop of elephants in Antigonus's army. Their position, as it would seem, was between the phalanx and the Gauls. This being the state of things, and Pyrrhus coming up to the attack in the rear, would, of course, encounter first the Gauls, then the elephants, and, lastly, the most formidable of all, the phalanx itself.

Pyrrhus advanced to the attack of the Gauls with the utmost fury, and, though they made a very determined resistance, they were soon overpowered and almost all cut to pieces. The troop of elephants came next. The army of Pyrrhus, flushed with their victory over the Gauls, pressed eagerly on, and soon so surrounded the elephants and hemmed them in, that the keepers of them perceived that all hope of resistance was vain. They surrendered without an effort to defend themselves. The phalanx now remained. It had hastily changed its front, and it stood on the defensive. Pyrrhus advanced toward it with his forces, bringing his men up in array in front of the long lines of spears, and paused. The bristling monster remained immovable, evincing no disposition to advance against its enemy, but awaiting, apparently, an attack. Pyrrhus rode out in front of his lines and surveyed the body of Macedonians before him. He found that he knew the officers personally, having served with them before in the wars in which he had been engaged in Macedon in former years. He saluted them, calling them by name. They were pleased with being thus remembered and recognized by a personage so renowned. Pyrrhus urged them to abandon Antigonus, who had, as he maintained, no just title to the crown, and whose usurped power he was about to overthrow, and invited them to enter into his service, as the ancient and rightful sovereign of their country. The officers seemed much disposed to listen to these overtures; in fine, they soon decided to accede to them. The phalanx went over to Pyrrhus's side in a body, and Antigonus, being thus deprived of his last remaining support, left the field in company with a few personal followers, and fled for his life.

Of course, Pyrrhus found himself at once in complete possession of the Macedonian kingdom. Antigonus did not, indeed, entirely give up the contest. He retreated toward the coast, where he contrived to hold possession, for a time, of a few maritime towns; but his power as King of Macedon was gone. Some few of the interior cities attempted, for a time, to resist Pyrrhus's rule, but he soon overpowered them. Some of the cities that he thus conquered he garrisoned with Gauls.

Of course, after such a revolution as this, a great deal was required to be done to settle the affairs of the government on their new footing, and to make the kingdom secure in the hands of the conqueror; but no one in the least degree acquainted with the character and tendencies of Pyrrhus's mind could expect that he would be at all disposed to attend to these duties. He had neither the sagacity to plan nor the steadiness of purpose to execute such measures. He could conquer, but that was all. To secure the results of his conquests was utterly beyond his power.

In fact, far from making such a use of his power as to strengthen his position, and establish a permanent and settled government, he so administered the affairs of state, or, rather, he so neglected them, that very soon an extended discontent and disaffection began to prevail. The Gauls, whom he had left as garrisons in the conquered cities, governed them in so arbitrary a manner, and plundered them so recklessly, as to produce extreme irritation among the people. They complained earnestly to Pyrrhus. Pyrrhus paid little attention to their representations. To fight a battle with an open enemy on the field was always a pleasure to him; but to meet and grapple with difficulties of this kind— to hear complaints, and listen to evidence, and discuss and consider remedies, was all weariness and toil to him.

What he would have done, and what would have been the end of his administration in Macedon, had he been left to himself, can not now be known; for, very fortunately, as he deemed it, he was suddenly relieved of all the embarrassment in which he was gradually getting involved, as he had often been relieved in similar circumstances before, by an invitation which came to him just at this time to embark in a new military enterprise, which would draw him away from the country altogether. It is scarcely necessary to say that Pyrrhus accepted the invitation with the most eager alacrity. The circumstances of the case will be explained in the next chapter.

11

Sparta

B.C. 1000-272

Sparta.—Some account of the city.—The Spartan kings.—Origin of the system.—Oracle at Delphi.—A difficulty.—The two lines of kings.—A diarchy.—Dissensions.—Lycurgus.—His family.—Death of his father.—Lycurgus assumes the crown.—Atrocious proposal.—Plan arranged for disposing of the child.—Generous conduct of Lycurgus.—Serious difficulties encountered.—Resentment of the queen.—Lycurgus resolves on exiling himself from Sparta.—Adventures of Lycurgus during his absence.—Account of Charilaus.—His inefficiency.—Discontent of the people.—Lycurgus is invited to return.—He finally complies.—He consults the oracle at Delphi.—The response.—Charilaus is terrified.—He flies to a sanctuary.—Nature and effects of the institutions of Lycurgus.—The character and spirit of the Spartans.—Message sent to Pyrrhus.—Account of Cleonymus.—Areus becomes king.—Affair of Cleonymus and Chelidonis.—Appeal to Pyrrhus.—Pyrrhus determines to march into Greece.

THE war in which Pyrrhus was invited to engage, at the time referred to at the close of the last chapter, arose out of a domestic quarrel in one of the royal families of Sparta. Sparta was one of the principal cities of the Peloponnesus, and the capital of a very powerful and warlike kingdom. The institutions of government in this commonwealth were very peculiar, and among the most extraordinary of them all was the arrangement made in respect to the kingly power. There were two dynasties, or lines of kings, reigning conjointly. The division of power between the two incumbents who reigned at any one time may have been somewhat similar to that made in Rome between the consuls. But the system differed from that of the consular government in the fact that the Spartan kings were not elected magistrates, like the Roman consuls, but hereditary sovereigns, deriving their power from their ancestors, each in his own line.

The origin of this extraordinary system was said to be this: at a very early period of the Spartan history, a king died suddenly, leaving two children twins, as his heirs, but without designating either one of them as his successor. The Spartans then applied to the mother of the two children to know which of them was the first-born. She pretended that she could not tell. They then applied to the oracle at Delphi, asking what they should do. The response of the oracle directed them to make both the children kings, but to bestow the highest honors upon the oldest. By this answer the Spartans were only partially relieved from their dilemma; for, under the directions of the oracle, the necessity of determining the question of priority in respect to the birth of the two children remained, without any light or guidance being afforded them in respect to the mode of doing it.

At last some person suggested that a watch should be set over the mother, with a view to ascertain for which of her children she had the strongest affection. They supposed that she really knew which was the first-born, and that she would involuntarily give to the one whom she regarded in that light the precedence in the maternal services and duties which she rendered to the babes. This plan succeeded. It was discovered which was the first-born, and which was the younger; and the Spartans, accordingly, made both the children kings, but gave the highest rank to the former, as the oracle had directed. The children both lived, and grew up to be men, and in due time were married. By a singular coincidence, they married twin-sisters. In the two families thus arising originated the

Spartan lines of kings that reigned jointly over the kingdom for many successive generations. To express this extraordinary system of government, it has sometimes been said that Sparta, though governed by kings, was not a monarchy, but a *diarchy*.

The diarchy, however, as might have been expected, was found not to work very successfully in practice. Various dissensions and difficulties arose; and at length, about two hundred years after the original establishment of the two lines, the kingdom became almost wholly disorganized. At this juncture the celebrated lawgiver Lycurgus arose. He framed a system of laws and regulations for the kingdom, which were immediately put in force, and resulted not only in restoring the public affairs to order at the time, but were the means, in the end, of raising Sparta to the highest condition of prosperity and renown.

Lycurgus was indebted for his success in the measures which he adopted not merely to the sagacity which he exercised in framing them, and the energy with which he carried them into effect: he occupied personally a very peculiar position, which afforded him great facilities for the performance of his work. He was a member of one of the royal families, being a younger son of one of the kings. He had an elder brother named Polydectes. His father died suddenly, from a stab that he received in a fray. He was not personally engaged in the fray himself as one of the combatants, but only went into it to separate other persons, who had by some means become involved in a sudden quarrel. In the struggle, he received a stab from a kitchen knife, with which one of the combatants was armed, and immediately died.

Polydectes, of course, being the eldest son, succeeded to the throne. He, however, very soon died, leaving a wife, but no children. About eight months after his death, however, a child was born to his widow, and this child, according to the then received principles of hereditary descent, was entitled to succeed his father.

As, however, at the time of Polydectes's death the child was not born, Lycurgus, the brother, was then apparently the heir. He accordingly assumed the government—so far as the government devolved upon the line to which his brother had belonged—intending only to hold it in the interim, and to give it up ultimately when the proper heir should appear. In the mean time, the widow supposed very naturally that he would like to retain the power permanently. She was herself also ambitious of reigning as queen; and she accordingly made to Lycurgus the atrocious and unnatural proposal to destroy the life of her child, on condition that he would marry her, and allow her to share the kingdom with him. Lycurgus was much shocked at receiving such a proposition, but he deemed it best, for the time being, to appear to accede to it. He accordingly represented to the queen that it would not be best for her to make the attempt which she had proposed, lest she should thereby endanger her own safety. "Wait," said he, "and let me know as soon as the child is born; then leave every thing to me. I will do myself whatever is required to be done."

Lycurgus, moreover, had attendants, provided with orders to keep themselves in readiness when the child should be born, and, if it proved to be a son, to bring the babe to him immediately, wherever he might be, or however he might be engaged. If it proved to be a daughter, they were to leave it in the hands of the woman who had charge of the queen. The babe proved to be a son. The officers took it, accordingly, and brought it at once to Lycurgus. The unnatural mother, of course, understood that it was taken away from her to be destroyed, and she acquiesced in the supposed design, in order, by sacrificing her child, to perpetuate her own queenly dignity and power. Lycurgus, however, was intending to conduct the affair to a very different result.

At the time when the attendants brought the new-born babe to Lycurgus's house, Lycurgus was engaged with a party of friends whom he had invited to a festival. These friends consisted of nobles, generals, ministers of state, and other principal personages of the Spartan commonwealth, whom Lycurgus had thus assembled in anticipation, probably, of what was to take place. The attendants had been ordered to bring the child to him without delay, wherever they might find him. They accordingly came into the apartment where Lycurgus and his friends were assembled, bringing the infant with them in their arms. Lycurgus received him, and holding him up before the company, called out to them, in a loud voice, "Spartans, I present to you your new-born king!" The people received the young prince with the most extravagant demonstrations of joy; and Lycurgus named him Charilaus, which means, "Dear to the people."

The conduct of Lycurgus on this occasion was thought to be very generous and noble, since by bringing the child forward as the true heir to the crown, he surrendered at once all his own pretensions to the inheritance, and made himself a private citizen. Very few of the sons of kings, either in ancient or modern times, would have pursued such a course. But, though in respect to his position, he abased himself by thus descending from his place upon the throne to the rank of a private citizen, he exalted himself very highly in respect to influence and character. He was at once made protector of the person of the child and regent of the realm during the young king's minority; and all the people of the city, applauding the noble deed which he had performed, began to entertain toward him feelings of the highest respect and veneration.

It proved, however, that there were yet very serious difficulties, which he was destined to meet and surmount before the way should be fully open for the performance of the great work for which he afterward became so renowned. Although the people generally of Sparta greatly applauded the conduct of Lycurgus, and placed the utmost confidence in him, there were still a few who hated and opposed him. Of course, the queen herself, whose designs he had thwarted, was extremely indignant at having been thus deceived. Not only was her own personal ambition disappointed by the failure of her design, but her womanly pride was fatally wounded in having been rejected by Lycurgus in the offer which she had made to become his wife. She and her friends, therefore, were implacably hostile to him. She had a brother, named Leonidas, who warmly espoused her cause. Leonidas quarreled openly with Lycurgus. He addressed him one day, in the presence of several witnesses, in a very violent and threatening manner. "I know very well," said he, "that your seeming disinterestedness, and your show of zeal for the safety and welfare of the young king, are all an empty pretense. You are plotting to destroy him, and to raise yourself to the throne in his stead; and if we wait a short time, we shall see you accomplishing the results at which you are really aiming, in your iniquitous and hypocritical policy."

On hearing these threats and denunciations, Lycurgus, instead of making an angry reply to them, began at once calmly to consider what it would be best for him to do. He reflected that the life of the child was uncertain, notwithstanding every precaution which he might make for the preservation of it; and if by any casualty it should die, his enemies might charge him with having secretly murdered it. He resolved, therefore, to remove at once and forever all possible suspicion, present or prospective, of the purity of his motives, by withdrawing altogether from Sparta until the child should come of age. He accordingly made arrangements for placing the young king under protectors who could not be suspected of collusion with him for any guilty purpose, and also organized an administration to govern the country until the king should be of age. Having taken these steps, he bade Sparta farewell, and set out upon a long and extended course of travels.

He was gone from his native land many years, during which period he visited all the principal states and kingdoms of the earth, employing himself, wherever he went, in studying the history, the government, and the institutions of the countries through which he journeyed, and in visiting and conversing with all the most distinguished men. He went first to Crete, a large island which lay south of the Ægean Sea, its western extremity being not far from the coast of Peloponnesus. After remaining for some time in Crete, visiting all its principal cities, and making himself thoroughly acquainted with its history and condition, he sailed for Asia Minor, and visited all the chief capitals there. From Asia Minor he went to Egypt, and, after finishing his observations and studies in the cities of the Nile, he journeyed westward, and passed through all the countries lying on the northern coast of Africa, and then from Africa he crossed over into Spain. He remained long enough in each place that he visited to make himself very thoroughly acquainted with its philosophy, its government, its civilization, its state of progress in respect to the arts and usages of social life—with every thing, in fact, which could have a bearing upon national prosperity and welfare.

In the mean time, the current of affairs at Sparta flowed by no means smoothly. As years rolled on, and the young prince, Charilaus, advanced toward the period of manhood, he became involved in various difficulties, which greatly embarrassed and perplexed him. He was of a very amiable and gentle disposition, but was wholly destitute of the strength and energy of character required for the station in which he was placed. Disagreements arose between him and the other king. They both quarreled, too, with their nobles and with the people. The people did not respect them, and gradually learned to despise their authority. They remembered the efficiency and the success of Lycurgus's government, and the regularity and order which had marked the whole course of public affairs during his administration. They appreciated now, too, more fully than before, the noble personal qualities which Lycurgus had evinced—his comprehensiveness of view, his firmness of purpose, his disinterestedness, his generosity; and they contrasted the lofty sentiments and principles which had always governed him with the weakness, the childishness, and the petty ambition of their actual kings. In a word, they all wished that Lycurgus would return.

Even the kings themselves participated in this wish. They perceived that their affairs were getting into confusion, and began to feel apprehension and anxiety. Lycurgus received repeated messages from them and from the people of Sparta, urging him to return, but he declined to accept these proposals, and went on with his travels and his studies as before.

At last, however, the Spartans sent a formal embassy to Lycurgus, representing to him the troubled condition of public affairs in Sparta, and the dangers which threatened the commonwealth, and urging him in the most pressing manner to return. These embassadors, in their interview with Lycurgus, told him that they had kings, indeed, at Sparta, so far as birth, and title, and the wearing of royal robes would go, but as for any royal qualities beyond this mere outside show, they had seen nothing of the kind since Lycurgus had left them.

Lycurgus finally concluded to comply with the request. He returned to Sparta. Here he employed himself for a time in making a careful examination into the state of the country, and in conversing with the principal men of influence in the city, and renewing his acquaintance with them. At length he formed a plan for an entire organization of the government. He proposed this plan to the principal men, and, having obtained the consent of a sufficient number of them to the leading provisions of his new constitution, he began to take measures for the public promulgation and establishment of it.

The first step was to secure a religious sanction for his proceedings, in order to inspire the common people with a feeling of reverence and awe for his authority. He accordingly left Sparta, saying that he was going to consult the oracle at Delphi. In due time he returned, bringing with him the response of the oracle. The response was as follows:

"Lycurgus is beloved of the gods, and is himself divine. The laws which he has framed are perfect, and under them a commonwealth shall arise which shall hereafter become the most famous in the world."

This response, having been made known in Sparta, impressed every one with a very high sense of the authority of Lycurgus, and disposed all classes of people to acquiesce in the coming change. Lycurgus did not, however, rely entirely on this disposition. When the time came for organizing the new government, he stationed an armed force in the market-place one morning at a very early hour, so that the people, when they came forth, as usual, into the streets, found that Lycurgus had taken military possession of the city. The first feeling was a general excitement and alarm. Charilaus, the king, who, it seems, had not been consulted in these movements at all, was very much terrified. He supposed that an insurrection had taken place against his authority, and that his life was in danger. To save himself, he fled to one of the temples as to a sanctuary. Lycurgus sent to him, informing him that those engaged in the revolution which had taken place intended no injury to him, either in respect to his person or his royal prerogatives. By these assurances the fears of Charilaus were allayed, and thenceforth he co-operated with Lycurgus in carrying his measures into effect.

This is not the place for a full account of the plan of government which Lycurgus introduced, nor of the institutions which gradually grew up under it. It is sufficient to say that the system which he adopted was celebrated throughout the world during the period of its continuance, and has since been celebrated in every age, as being the most stern and rugged social system that was ever framed. The commonwealth of Sparta became, under the institutions of Lycurgus, one great camp. The nation was a nation of soldiers. Every possible device was resorted to to inure all classes of the population, the young and the old, the men and the women, the rich and the poor, to every species of hardship and privation. The only qualities that were respected or cultivated were such stern virtues as courage, fortitude, endurance, insensibility to pain and grief, and contempt for all the pleasures of wealth and luxury. Lycurgus did not write out his system. He would not allow it to be written out. He preferred to put it in operation, and then leave it to perpetuate itself, as a matter of usage and precedent. Accordingly, after fully organizing the government on the plan which he had arranged, and announcing the laws, and establishing the customs by which he intended that the ordinary course of social life should be regulated, he determined to withdraw from the field and await the result. He therefore informed the people that he was going away again on another journey, and that he would leave the carrying forward of the government which he had framed for them and initiated in their hands; and he required of them a solemn oath that they would make no change in the system until he returned. In doing this, his secret intention was *never* to return.

Such was the origin, and such the general character of the Spartan government. In the time of Pyrrhus, the system had been in operation for about five hundred years.[O] During this period the state passed through many and various vicissitudes. It engaged in wars, offensive and defensive; it passed through many calamitous and trying scenes, suffering, from time to time, under the usual ills which, in those days, so often disturbed the peace and welfare of nations. But during all this time, the commonwealth retained in a very striking degree the extraordinary marks and characteristics which the institutions of Lycurgus had enstamped upon it. The Spartans still were terrible in the estimation of all mankind, so stern and indomitable was the spirit which they manifested in all the enterprises in which they engaged.

[Footnote O: The precise time at which the events connected with the early history of Sparta really occurred is not satisfactorily determined, so that the dates placed at the heads of the pages can only be regarded as approximations.]

It was from Sparta that the message came to Pyrrhus asking his assistance in a war that was then waging there. The war originated in a domestic quarrel which arose in the family of one of the lines of kings. The name of the prince who made application to Pyrrhus was Cleonymus. He was a younger son of one of the Spartan kings. He had had an older brother named Acrotatus. The crown, of course, would have devolved on this brother, if he had been living when the father died. But he was not. He died before his father, leaving a son, however, named Areus, as his heir. Areus, of course, claimed the throne when his grandfather died. He was not young himself at this time. He had advanced beyond the period of middle life, and had a son who had grown up to maturity.

Cleonymus was very unwilling to acquiesce in the accession of Areus to the throne. He was himself the son of the king who had died, while Areus was only the grandson. He maintained, therefore, that he had the highest claim to the succession. He was, however, overruled, and Areus assumed the crown.

Soon after his accession, Areus left Sparta and went to Crete, intrusting the government of his kingdom, in the mean time, to his son. The name of this son was Acrotatus. Cleonymus, of course, looked with a particularly evil eye upon this young man, and soon began to form designs against him. At length, after the lapse of a considerable period, during which various events occurred which can not be here described, a circumstance took place which excited the hostility which Cleonymus felt for Acrotatus to the highest degree. The circumstances were these:

Cleonymus, though far advanced in life, married, about the time that the events occurred which we are here describing, a very young lady named Chelidonis. Chelidonis was a princess of the royal line, and was a lady of great personal beauty. She, however, had very little affection for her husband, and at length Acrotatus, who was young and attractive in person, succeeded in winning her love, and enticing her away from her husband. This affair excited the mind of Cleonymus to a perfect phrensy of jealousy and rage. He immediately left Sparta, and, knowing well the character and disposition of Pyrrhus, he proceeded northward to Macedon, laid his case before Pyrrhus, and urged him to fit out an expedition and march to the Peloponnesus, with a view of aiding him to put down the usurpers, as he called them, and to establish him on the throne of Sparta instead. Pyrrhus immediately saw that the conjuncture opened before him a prospect of a very brilliant campaign, in a field entirely new, and he at once determined to embark forthwith in the enterprise. He resolved, accordingly, to abandon his interests in Macedon and march into Greece.

12

The Last Campaign of Pyrrhus

B.C. 272

Pyrrhus makes preparations for his campaign.—Pyrrhus's designs.—Excitement in Greece.—Pyrrhus's army advances toward Sparta.—Embassadors.—Pyrrhus arrives at Sparta.—He postpones the attack.—Plans of the Spartans.—They propose to remove the women.—The women send a delegation into the senate-chamber.—Preparations for receiving Cleonymus.—His wife.—The Spartans resolve to attack Pyrrhus in the morning. —Ditch dug.—Ramparts raised.—The labors of the women.—Digging the trench.—Citizens at work all night.—The women assist.—Effect of the trench.—The wagons.—Ptolemy, the son of Pyrrhus, removes the wagons. —The triumph of Acrotatus.—Pyrrhus's dream.—The dream produces no effect.—Pyrrhus tries another plan.—The battle.—Work of the women.— Pyrrhus leads the troops forward.—Pyrrhus's horse is wounded.—Pyrrhus himself in great danger.—The army retires.—Areus and Acrotatus.— Areus comes to succor the city.—Pyrrhus receives a new invitation.—Argos. —Pyrrhus leaves Sparta, and is pursued.—Death of Ptolemy.—Combat with Evalcus.—Pyrrhus's revenge.—Pyrrhus before the walls of Argos.—A stratagem.—Attempt of the elephants to enter the city.—Consternation of the inhabitants of Argos.—Confusion of the soldiers.—Pyrrhus waits for morning.—The bronze statue.—Ancient prophecy.—Pyrrhus's alarm.— He resolves to retreat from the city.—Pyrrhus finds the streets blocked up.

—Dreadful confusion.—The fallen elephant in the gateway.—Pyrrhus is greatly alarmed.—He lays aside his plume.—He is struck by a tile thrown down upon him.—His dreadful death.—The head borne away.—Summary of Pyrrhus's character.—Conclusion.

IMMEDIATELY on receiving the invitation of Cleonymus, Pyrrhus commenced making preparations on a very extensive scale for the intended campaign. He gathered all the troops that he could command, both from Macedon and Epirus. He levied taxes and contributions, provided military stores of every kind, and entered into all the other arrangements required for such an enterprise. These preliminary operations required a considerable time, so that he was not ready to commence his march until the following year. When all was ready, he found that his force consisted of twenty-five thousand foot, two thousand horse, and a troop of twenty-four elephants. He had two sons, neither of whom, it would seem, was old enough to be intrusted with the command, either in Macedon or Epirus, during his absence, and he accordingly determined to take them with him. Their names were Ptolemy and Helenus. Pyrrhus himself at this time was about forty-five years of age.

Although in this expedition Cleonymus supposed that Pyrrhus was going into Greece only as his ally, and that the sole object of the war was to depose Areus and place Cleonymus on the throne in his stead, Pyrrhus himself entertained far different designs. His intention was, while invading the country in Cleonymus's name, to overrun and conquer it all, with a view of adding it to his own dominions. Of course, he gave no intimation to Cleonymus that he entertained any such designs.

The approach of Pyrrhus naturally produced great excitement and commotion in Sparta. His fame as a military commander was known throughout the world; and the invasion of their country by such a conqueror, at the head of so large a force, was calculated to awaken great alarm among the people. The Spartans, however, were not much accustomed to be alarmed. They immediately began to make preparations to defend themselves. They sent forward an embassage to meet Pyrrhus on the way, and demand wherefore he was coming. Pyrrhus made evasive and dishonest replies. He was not intending, he said, to commit any hostilities against Sparta. His business was with certain other cities of the Peloponnesus, which had been for some time under a foreign yoke, and which he was now coming to free. The Spartans were not deceived by these protestations, but time was gained, and this was Pyrrhus's design.

His army continued to advance, and in its progress began to seize and plunder towns belonging to the Spartan territory. The Spartans sent embassadors again, demanding what these proceedings meant. The embassadors charged it upon Pyrrhus, that, contrary to the laws and usages of nations, he was making war upon them without having previously declared war.

"And do you Spartans," said Pyrrhus, in reply, "always tell the world whatever you are going to do before you do it?" Such a rejoinder was virtually acknowledging that the object of the expedition was an attack on Sparta itself. The embassadors so understood it, and bid the invader defiance.

"Let there be war, then," said they, "if you will have it so. We do not fear you, whether you are a god or a man. If you are a god, you will not be disposed to do us any injury, for we have never injured you. If you are a man, you can not harm us, for we can produce men in Sparta able to meet any other man whatever."

The embassadors then returned to Sparta, and the people immediately pushed forward with all diligence their preparations for putting the city in an attitude of defense.

Pyrrhus continued his march, and at length, toward evening, approached the walls of the city. Cleonymus, who knew well what sort of enemies they had to deal with, urgently recommended that an assault should be made that night, supposing that the Spartans would succeed in making additional defenses if the attack were postponed until the morning. Pyrrhus, however, was disposed not to make the attack until the following day. He felt perfectly sure of his prize, and was, accordingly, in no haste to seize it. He thought, it was said, that if the attack were made in the night, the soldiers would plunder the city, and thus he should lose a considerable part of the booty which he hoped otherwise to secure for himself. He could control them better in the daytime. He accordingly determined to remain in his camp, without the city, during the night, and to advance to the assault in the morning. So he ordered the tents to be pitched on the plain, and sat quietly down.

In the mean time, great activity prevailed within the walls. The senate was convened, and was engaged in debating and deciding the various questions that necessarily arise in such an emergency. A plan was proposed for removing the women from the city, in order to save them from the terrible fate which would inevitably await them, should the army of Pyrrhus be successful on the following day. It was thought that they might go out secretly on the side opposite to that on which Pyrrhus was encamped, and thence be conducted to the sea-shore, where they might be conveyed in ships and galleys to the island of Crete, which, as will appear from the map, was situated at no great distance from the Spartan coast. By this means the mothers and daughters, it was thought, would be saved, whatever might be the fate of the husbands and brothers. The news that the senate were discussing such a plan as this was soon spread abroad among the people. The women were aroused to the most strenuous opposition against this plan. They declared that they never would seek safety for themselves by going away, and leaving their fathers, husbands, and brothers in such danger. They commissioned one of their number, a princess named Archidamia, to make known to the senate the views which they entertained of this proposal. Archidamia went boldly into the senate-chamber, with a drawn sword in her hand, and there arrested the discussion in which the senators were engaged by demanding how they could entertain such an opinion of the women of Sparta as to suppose that they could survive the destruction of the city and the death of all whom they loved. They did not wish to be saved, she said, unless all could be saved together; and she implored the senate to abandon at once all ideas of sending them away, and allow them, instead, to take their share in the necessary labors required for the defense of the city. The senate yielded to this appeal, and, abandoning the design which they had entertained of sending the women away, turned their attention immediately to plans of defense.

While these earnest consultations and discussions were going on in the senate, and in the streets and dwellings of the city, there was one place which presented a scene of excitement of a very different kind—namely, the palace of Cleonymus. There all were in a state of eager anticipation, expecting the speedy arrival of their master. The domestics believed confidently that an attack would be made upon the city that night by the combined army of Cleonymus and Pyrrhus; and presuming that it would be successful, they supposed that their master, as soon as the troops should obtain possession of the city, would come home at once to his own house, bringing his distinguished ally with him. They busied themselves, therefore, in adorning and preparing the apartments of the house, and in making ready a splendid entertainment, in order that they might give to Cleonymus and his friend a suitable reception when they should arrive.

Chelidonis, however, the young and beautiful, but faithless wife of Cleonymus, was not there. She had long since left her husband's dwelling, and now she was full of suspense and anxiety in respect to his threatened return. If the city should be taken, she knew very well that she must necessarily fall again into her husband's power, and she determined that she never would fall into his power again alive. So she retired to her apartment, and there putting a rope around her neck, and making all other necessary preparations, she awaited the issue of the battle, resolved to destroy herself the moment she should hear tidings that Pyrrhus had gained the victory.

In the mean time, the military leaders of the Spartans were engaged in strengthening the defenses, and in making all the necessary preparations for the ensuing conflict. They did not, however, intend to remain within the city, and await the attack of the assailants there. With the characteristic fearlessness of the Spartan character, they determined, when they found that Pyrrhus was not intending to attack the city that night, that they would themselves go out to meet him in the morning.

One reason, however, for this determination doubtless was, that the city was not shut in with substantial walls and defenses, like most of the other cities of Greece, as it was a matter of pride with the Spartans to rely on their own personal strength and courage for protection, rather than on artificial bulwarks and towers. Still, such artificial aids were not wholly despised, and they now determined to do what was in their power in this respect, by throwing up a rampart of earth, under cover of the darkness of the night, along the line over which the enemy must march in attacking the city. This work was accordingly begun. They would not, however, employ the soldiers in the work, or any strong and able-bodied men capable of bearing arms. They wished to reserve the strength of all these for the more urgent and dreadful work of the following day. The ditch was accordingly dug, and the ramparts raised by the boys, the old men, and especially by the women. The women of all ranks in the city went out and toiled all night at this labor, having laid aside half their clothes, that their robes might not hinder them in the digging. The reader, however, must not, in his imagination, invest these fair laborers with the delicate forms, and gentle manners, and timid hearts which are generally deemed characteristic of women, for the Spartan females were trained expressly, from their earliest life, to the most rough and bold exposures and toils. They were inured from infancy to hardihood, by being taught to contend in public wrestlings and games, to endure every species of fatigue and exposure, and to despise every thing like gentleness and delicacy. In a word, they were little less masculine in appearance and manners than the men; and accordingly, when Archidamia went into the senate-chamber with a drawn sword in her hand, and there, boldly facing the whole assembly, declared that the women would on no account consent to leave the city, she acted in a manner not at all inconsistent with what at Sparta was considered the proper position and character of her sex. In a word, the Spartan women were as bold and stern, and almost as formidable, as the men.

All night long the work of excavation went on. Those who were too young or too feeble to work were employed in going to and fro, carrying tools where they were required, or bringing food and drink to those who were digging in the trench, while the soldiers remained quietly at rest within the city, awaiting the duties which were to devolve upon them in the morning. The trench was made wide and deep enough to impede the passage of the elephants and of the cavalry, and it was guarded at the ends by wagons, the wheels of which were half buried in the ground at the places chosen for them, in order to render them immovable. All this work was performed in such silence and secrecy that it met with no interruption from Pyrrhus's camp, and the whole was completed before the morning dawned.

As soon as it began to be light, the camp of Pyrrhus was in motion. All was excitement and commotion, too, within the city. The soldiers assumed their arms and formed in array. The women gathered around them while they were making these preparations, assisting them to buckle on their armor, and animating them with words of sympathy and encouragement. "How glorious it will be for you," said they, "to gain a victory here in the precincts of the city, where we can all witness and enjoy your triumph; and even if you fall in the contest, your mothers and your wives are close at hand to receive you to their arms, and to soothe and sustain you in your dying struggles!"

When all was ready, the men marched forth to meet the advancing columns of Pyrrhus's army, and the battle soon began. Pyrrhus soon found that the trench which the Spartans had dug in the night was destined greatly to obstruct his intended operations. The horse and the elephants could not cross it at all; and even the men, if they succeeded in getting over the ditch, were driven back when attempting to ascend the rampart of earth which had been formed along the side of it, by the earth thrown up in making the excavation, for this earth was loose and steep, and afforded them no footing. Various attempts were made

THE HISTORY OF PYRRHUS

to dislodge the wagons that had been fixed into the ground at the ends of the trench, but for a time all these efforts were fruitless. At last, however, Ptolemy, the son of Pyrrhus, came very near succeeding. He had the command of a force of about two thousand Gauls, and with this body he made a circuit, so as to come upon the line of wagons in such a manner as to give him a great advantage in attacking them. The Spartans fought very resolutely in defense of them; but the Gauls gradually prevailed, and at length succeeded in dragging several of the wagons up out of the earth. All that they thus extricated they drew off out of the way, and threw them into the river.

Seeing this, young Acrotatus, the prince whom Areus his father, now absent, as the reader will recollect, in Crete, had left in command in Sparta when he went away, hastened to interpose. He placed himself at the head of a small band of two or three hundred men, and, crossing the city on the other side, he went unobserved, and then, making a circuit, came round and attacked the Gauls, who were at work on the wagons in the rear. As the Gauls had already a foe in front nearly strong enough to cope with them, this sudden assault from behind entirely turned the scale. They were driven away in great confusion. This feat being accomplished, Acrotatus came back at the head of his detachment into the city, panting and exhausted with the exertions he had made, and covered with blood. He was received there with the loudest applause and acclamations. The women gathered around him, and overwhelmed him with thanks and congratulations. "Go to Chelidonis," said they, "and rest. She ought to be yours. You have deserved her. How we envy her such a lover!"

The contest continued all the day, and when night came on Pyrrhus found that he had made no sensible progress in the work of gaining entrance into the city. He was, however, now forced to postpone all further efforts till the following day. At the proper time he retired to rest, but he awoke very early in the morning in a state of great excitement; and, calling up some of the officers around him, he related to them a remarkable dream which he had had during the night, and which, he thought, presaged success to the efforts which they were to make on the following day. He had seen, he said, in his dream, a flash of lightning dart from the sky upon Sparta, and set the whole city on fire. This, he argued, was a divine omen which promised them certain success; and he called upon the generals to marshal the troops and prepare for the onset, saying, "We are sure of victory now."

Whether Pyrrhus really had had such a dream, or whether he fabricated the story for the purpose of inspiring anew the courage and confidence of his men, which, as would naturally be supposed, might have been somewhat weakened by the ill success of the preceding day, can not be absolutely ascertained. Whichever it was, it failed wholly of its intended effect. Pyrrhus's generals said, in reply, that the omen was adverse, and not propitious, for it was one of the fundamental principles of haruspicial science that lightning made sacred whatever it touched. It was forbidden even to step upon the ground where a thunder-bolt had fallen; and they ought to consider, therefore, that the descent of the lightning upon Sparta, as figured to Pyrrhus in the dream, was intended to mark the city as under the special protection of heaven, and to warn the invaders not to molest it. Finding thus that the story of his vision produced a different effect from the one he had intended, Pyrrhus changed his ground, and told his generals that no importance whatever was to be attached to visions and dreams. They might serve, he argued, very well to amuse the ignorant and superstitious, but wise men should be entirely above being influenced by them in any way. "You have something better than these things to trust in," said he. "You have arms in your hands, and you have Pyrrhus for your leader. This is proof enough for you that you are destined to conquer."

How far these assurances were found effectual in animating the courage of the generals we do not know; but the result did not at all confirm Pyrrhus's vain-glorious predictions. During the first part of the day, indeed, he made great progress, and for a time it appeared probable that the city was about to fall into his hands. The plan of his operations was first to fill up the ditch which the Spartans had made; the soldiers throwing into it for this purpose great quantities of materials of every kind, such as earth, stones, fagots, trunks of trees, and whatever came most readily to hand. They used in this work immense quantities of dead bodies, which they found scattered over the plain, the results of the conflict of the preceding day. By means of the horrid bridging thus made, the troops attempted to make their way across the ditch, while the Spartans, formed on the top of the rampart of earth on the inner side of it, fought desperately to repel them. All this time the women were passing back and forth between them and the city, bringing out water and refreshments to sustain the fainting strength of the men, and carrying home the wounded and dying, and the bodies of the dead.

The Charge.

At last a considerable body of troops, consisting of a division that was under the personal charge of Pyrrhus himself, succeeded in breaking through the Spartan lines, at a point near one end of the rampart which had been thrown up. When the men found that they had forced their way through, they raised loud shouts of exultation and triumph, and immediately rushed forward toward the city. For a moment it seemed that for the Spartans all was lost; but the tide of victory was soon suddenly turned by a very unexpected incident. An arrow pierced the breast of the horse on which Pyrrhus was riding, and gave the animal a fatal wound. The horse plunged and reared in his agony and terror, and then fell, throwing Pyrrhus to the ground. This occurrence, of course, arrested the whole troop in their progress. The horsemen wheeled suddenly about, and gathered around Pyrrhus to rescue him from his danger. This gave the Spartans time to rally, and to bring up their forces in such numbers that the Macedonian soldiers were glad to be able to make their way back again, bearing Pyrrhus with them beyond the lines. After recovering a little from the agitation produced by this adventure, Pyrrhus found that his troops, discouraged, apparently, by the fruitlessness of their efforts, and especially by this last misfortune, were beginning to lose their spirit and ardor, and were fighting feebly and falteringly all along the line. He concluded, therefore, that there was no longer any prospect of accomplishing his object that day, and that it would be better to save the remaining strength of his troops by withdrawing them from the field, rather than to discourage and enfeeble them still more by continuing what was now very clearly a useless struggle. He accordingly put a stop to the action, and the army retired to their encampment.

Before he had opportunity to make a third attempt, events occurred which entirely changed the whole aspect of the controversy. The reader will recollect that Areus, the king of Sparta, was absent in Crete at the time of Pyrrhus's arrival, and that the command of the army devolved, during his absence, on Acrotatus, his son; for the kings of the other line, for some reason or other, took a very small part in the public affairs of the city at this time, and are seldom mentioned in history. Areus, as soon as he heard of the Macedonian invasion, immediately collected a large force and set out on his return to Sparta, and he entered into the city at the head of two thousand men just after the second repulse which Acrotatus had given to their enemies. At the same time, too, another body of re-enforcements came in from Corinth, consisting of allies of the Spartans, gathered from the northern part of the Peloponnesus. The arrival of these troops in the city filled the Spartans with joy, and entirely dispelled their fears. They considered themselves as now entirely safe. The old men and the women, considering that their places were now abundantly supplied, thenceforth withdrew from all active participation in the contest, and retired to their respective homes, to rest and refresh themselves after their toils.

Notwithstanding this, however, Pyrrhus was not yet prepared to give up the contest. The immediate effect, in fact, of the arrival of the re-enforcements was to arouse his spirit anew, and to stimulate him to a fresh determination that he would not be defeated in his purpose, but that he would conquer the city at all hazards. He accordingly made several more desperate attempts, but they were wholly unsuccessful; and at length, after a series of losses and defeats, he was obliged to give up the contest and withdraw. He retired, accordingly, to some little distance from Sparta, where he established a permanent camp, subsisting his soldiers by plundering the surrounding country. He was vexed and irritated by the mortifications and disappointments which he had endured, and waited impatiently for an opportunity to seek revenge.

While he was thus pondering his situation, uncertain what to do next, he received one day a message from Argos, a city in the northern part of the Peloponnesus, asking him to come and take part in a contest which had been opened there. It seems that a civil war had broken out in that city, and one of the leaders, knowing the character of Pyrrhus, and his readiness to engage in any quarrel which was offered to him, had concluded to apply for his aid. Pyrrhus was, as usual, very ready to yield to this request. It afforded him, as similar proposals had so often done before, a plausible excuse for abandoning an enterprise in which he began to despair of being able to succeed. He immediately commenced his march to the northward. The Spartans, however, were by no means disposed to allow him to go off unmolested. They advanced with all the force they could command, and, though they were not powerful enough to engage him in a general battle, they harassed him and embarrassed his march in a very vexatious manner. They laid ambushes in the narrow defiles through which he had to pass; they cut off his detachments, and plundered and destroyed his baggage. Pyrrhus at length sent back a body of his guards under Ptolemy, his son, to drive them away. Ptolemy attacked the Spartans and fought them with great bravery, until at length, in the heat of the contest, a celebrated Cretan, of remarkable strength and activity, riding furiously up to Ptolemy, felled him to the ground, and killed him at a single blow. On seeing him fall, his detachment were struck with dismay, and, turning their backs on the Spartans, fled to Pyrrhus with the tidings.

Pyrrhus was, of course, excited to the highest pitch of phrensy at hearing what had occurred. He immediately placed himself at the head of a troop of horse, and galloped back to attack the Spartans and avenge the death of his son. He assaulted his enemies, when he reached the ground where they were posted, in the most furious manner, and killed great numbers of them in the conflict that ensued. At one time, he was for a short period in the most imminent danger. A Spartan, named Evalcus, who came up and engaged him hand to hand, aimed a blow at his head, which, although it failed of its intended effect, came down close in front of his body, as he sat upon his horse, and cut off the reins of the bridle. The instant after, Pyrrhus transfixed Evalcus with his spear. Of course, Pyrrhus had now no longer the control of his horse, and he accordingly leaped from him to the ground and fought on foot, while the Spartans gathered around, endeavoring to rescue and protect the body of Evalcus. A furious and most terrible contest ensued, in which many on both sides were slain. At length Pyrrhus made good his retreat from the scene, and the Spartans themselves finally withdrew. Pyrrhus having thus, by way of comfort for his grief, taken the satisfaction of revenge, resumed his march and went to Argos.

Arrived before the city, he found that there was an army opposed to him there, under the command of a general named Antigonus. His army was encamped upon a hill near the city, awaiting his arrival. The mind of Pyrrhus had become so chafed and irritated by the opposition which he had encountered, and the defeats, disappointments, and mortifications which he had endured, that he was full of rage and fury, and seemed to manifest the temper of a wild beast rather than that of a man. He sent a herald to the camp of Antigonus, angrily defying him, and challenging him to come down from his encampment and meet him in single combat on the plain. Antigonus very coolly replied that *time* was a weapon which he employed in his contests as well as the sword, and that he was not yet ready for a battle; adding, that if Pyrrhus was weary of his life, and very impatient to end it, there were plenty of modes by which he could accomplish his desire.

Pyrrhus remained for some days before the walls of Argos, during which time various negotiations took place between the people of the city and the several parties involved in the quarrel, with a view to an amicable adjustment of the dispute, in order to save the city from the terrors attendant upon a contest for the possession of it between such mighty armies. At length some sort of settlement was made, and both armies agreed to retire. Pyrrhus, however, had no intention of keeping his agreement. Having thrown the people of the city somewhat off their guard by his promise, he took occasion to advance stealthily to one of the gates at dead of night, and there, the gate being opened to him by a confederate within the city, he began to march his soldiers in. The troops were ordered to keep silence, and to step noiselessly, and thus a large body of Gauls gained admission, and posted themselves in the market-place without alarming or awakening the inhabitants. To render this story credible, we must suppose that the sentinels and guards had been previously gained over to Pyrrhus's side.

The foot-soldiers having thus made their entrance into the city, Pyrrhus undertook next to pass some of his elephants in. It was found, however, when they approached the gate, that they could not enter without having the towers first removed from their backs, as the gates were only high enough to admit the animals alone. The soldiers accordingly proceeded to take off the towers, and then the elephants were led in. The towers were then to be replaced. The work of taking down the towers, and then of putting them on again, which all had to be done in the dark, was attended with great difficulty and delay, and so much noise was unavoidably made in the operation, that at length the people in the surrounding houses took the alarm, and in a very short period the whole city was aroused. Eager gatherings were immediately held in all quarters. Pyrrhus pressed forward with all haste into the market-place, and posted himself there, arranging his elephants, his horse, and his foot in the manner best adapted to protect them from any attack that might be made. The people of Argos crowded into the citadel, and sent out immediately to Antigonus to come in to their aid. He at once put his camp in motion, and, advancing toward the walls with the main body, he sent in some powerful detachments of troops to co-operate with the inhabitants of the city. All these scenes occurring in the midst of the darkness of the night, the people having been awakened from their sleep by a sudden alarm, were attended, of course, by a dreadful panic and confusion; and, to complete the complication of horrors, Areus, with the Spartan army under his command, who had followed Pyrrhus in his approach to the city, and had been closely watching his movements ever since he had arrived, now burst in through the gates, and attacked the troops of his hated enemy in the streets, in the market-place, and wherever he could find them, with shouts, outcries, and imprecations, that made the whole city one widespread scene of unutterable confusion and terror.

The general confusion and terror, however, produced by the assaults of the Spartans were the only results that immediately followed them, for the troops soon found that no real progress could be made, and no advantage gained by this nocturnal warfare. The soldiers could not distinguish friends from foes. They could not see or hear their commander, or act with any concert or in any order. They were scattered about, and lost their way in narrow streets, or fell into drains or sewers, and all attempts on the part of the officers to rally them, or to control them in any way, were unavailing. At length, by common consent, all parties desisted from fighting, and awaited—all in an awful condition of uncertainty and suspense—the coming of the dawn.

Pyrrhus, as the objects that were around him were brought gradually into view by the gray light of the morning, was alarmed at seeing that the walls of the citadel were covered with armed men, and at observing various other indications, by which he was warned that there was a very powerful force opposed to him within the city. As the light increased, and brought the boundaries of the market-place where he posted himself into view, and revealed the various images and figures which had been placed there to adorn it, he was struck with consternation at the sight of one of the groups, as the outlines of it slowly made themselves visible. It was a piece of statuary, in bronze, representing a combat between a wolf and a bull. It seems that in former times some oracle or diviner had forewarned him that when he should see a wolf encountering a bull, he might know that the hour of his death was near. Of course, he had supposed that such a spectacle, if it was indeed true that he was ever destined to see it, could only be expected to appear in some secluded forest, or in some wide and unfrequented spot among the mountains. Perhaps, indeed, he had paid very little attention to the prophecy, and never expected that it would be literally realized. When, however, this group in bronze came out to view, it reminded him of the oracle, and the dreadful foreboding which its appearance awakened, connected with the anxiety and alarm naturally inspired by the situation in which he was placed, filled him with consternation. He feared that his hour was come, and his only solicitude now was to make good his retreat as soon as possible from the fatal dangers by which he seemed to be surrounded.

But how to escape was the difficulty. The gate was narrow, the body of troops with him was large, and he knew that in attempting to retire he would be attacked from all the streets in the vicinity, and from the tops of the houses and walls, and that his column would inevitably be thrown into disorder, and would choke up the gateway and render it wholly impassable, through their eagerness to escape and the confusion that would ensue. He accordingly sent out a messenger to his son Helenus, who remained all the time in command of the main body of the army, without the walls, directing him to come forward with all his force, and break down a portion of the wall adjoining the gateway, so as to open a free egress for his troops in their retreat from the city. He remained himself at his position in the market-place until time had elapsed sufficient, as he judged, for Helenus to have received his orders, and to have reached the gate in the execution of them; and then, being by this time hard pressed by his enemies, who began early in the morning to attack him on all quarters, he put his troops in motion, and in the midst of a scene of shouts, uproar, terror, and confusion indescribable, the whole body moved on toward the gate, expecting that, by the time they arrived there, Helenus would have accomplished his work, and that they should find a broad opening made, which would allow of an easy egress. Instead of this, however, they found, before they reached the gate, that the streets before them were entirely blocked up with an immense concourse of soldiers that were pouring tumultuously into the city. It seems that Helenus had, in some way or other, misunderstood the orders, and supposed that he was directed to enter the city himself, to re-enforce his father within the walls. The shock of the encounter produced by these opposing currents redoubled the confusion. Pyrrhus, and the officers with him, shouted out orders to the advancing soldiers of Helenus to fall back; but in the midst of the indescribable din and confusion that prevailed, no vociferation, however loud, could be heard. Nor, if the orders had been heard, could they have been obeyed, for the van of the coming column was urged forward irresistibly by the pressure of those behind, and the panic which by this time prevailed among the troops of Pyrrhus's command made them frantic and furious in their efforts to force their way onward and get out of the city. An awful scene of confusion and destruction ensued. Men pressed and trampled each other to death, and the air was filled with shrieks and cries of pain and terror. The destruction of life was very great, but it was produced almost entirely by the pressure and the confusion—men, horses, and elephants being mingled inextricably together in one vast living mass, which seemed, to those who looked down upon it from above, to be writhing and struggling in the most horrible contortions. There was no fighting, for there was no room for any one to strike a blow. If a man drew his sword or raised his pike, his arms were caught and pinioned immediately by the pressure around him, and he found himself utterly helpless. The injury, therefore, that was done, was the result almost altogether of the pressure and the struggles, and of the trampling of the elephants and the horses upon the men, and of the men upon each other.

The elephants added greatly to the confusion of the scene. One of the largest in the troop fell in the gateway, and lay there for some time on his side, unable to rise, and braying in a terrific manner. Another was excited to a phrensy by the loss of his master, who had fallen off from his head, wounded by a dart or a spear. The faithful animal turned around to save him. With his trunk he threw the men who were in the way off to the right hand and the left, and then, taking up the body of his master with his trunk, he placed it carefully upon his tusks, and then attempted to force a passage through the crowd, trampling down all who came in his way. History has awarded to this elephant a distinction which he well deserved, by recording his name. It was Nicon.

All this time Pyrrhus was near the rear of his troops, and thus was in some degree removed from the greatest severity of the pressure. He turned and fought, from time to time, with those who were pressing upon his line from behind. As the danger became more imminent, he took out from his helmet the plume by which he was distinguished from the other generals, and gave it to a friend who was near him, in order that he might be a less conspicuous mark for the shafts of his enemies. The combats, however, between his party and those who were harassing them in the rear were still continued; and at length, in one of them, a man of Argos wounded him, by throwing a javelin with so much force that the point of it passed through his breast-plate and entered his side.

Death of Pyrrhus

The wound was not dangerous, but it had the effect of maddening Pyrrhus against the man who had inflicted it, and he turned upon him with great fury, as if he were intending to annihilate him at a blow. He would very probably have killed the Greek, had it not been that just at that moment the mother of the man, by a very singular coincidence, was surveying the scene from a house-top which overlooked the street where these events were occurring. She immediately seized a heavy tile from the roof, and with all her strength hurled it into the street upon Pyrrhus just as he was striking the blow. The tile came down upon his head, and, striking the helmet heavily, it carried both helmet and head down together, and crushed the lower vertebræ of the neck at their junction with the spine.

Pyrrhus dropped the reins from his hands, and fell over from his horse heavily to the ground. It happened that no one knew him who saw him fall, for so great had been the crowd and confusion, that Pyrrhus had got separated from his immediate friends. Those who were near him, therefore, when he fell, pressed on, intent only on their own safety, and left him where he lay. At last a soldier of Antigonus's army, named Zopyrus, coming up to the spot, accompanied by several others of his party, looked upon the wounded man and recognized him as Pyrrhus. They lifted him up, and dragged him out of the street to a portico that was near. Zopyrus drew his sword, and raised it to cut off his prisoner's head. At this instant Pyrrhus opened his eyes, and rolled them up with such a horrid expression as to strike Zopyrus with terror. His arm consequently faltered in dealing the blow, so that he missed his aim, and instead of striking the neck, only wounded and mutilated the mouth and chin. He was obliged to repeat the stroke again and again before the neck was sundered. At length, however, the dreadful deed was done, and the head was severed from the body.

Very soon after this, Halcyoncus, the son of Antigonus, rode up to the spot, and after learning what had occurred, he asked the soldiers to lift up the head to him, that he might look at it a moment. As soon as it was within his reach, he seized it and rode away, in order to carry it to his father. He found his father sitting with his friends, and threw down the head at his feet, as a trophy which he supposed his father would rejoice to see. Antigonus was, however, in fact, extremely shocked at the spectacle. He reproved his son in the severest terms for his brutality, and then, sending for the mutilated trunk, he gave to the whole body an honorable burial.

That Pyrrhus was a man of great native power of mind, and of extraordinary capacity as a military leader, no one can deny. His capacity and genius were in fact so great, as to make him, perhaps, the most conspicuous example that the world has produced of the manner in which the highest power and the noblest opportunities may be wasted and thrown away. He accomplished nothing. He had no plan, no aim, no object, but obeyed every momentary impulse, and entered, without thought and without calculation, into any scheme that chance, or the ambitious designs of others, might lay before him. He succeeded in creating a vast deal of turmoil and war, in killing an immense number of men, and in conquering, though temporarily and to no purpose, a great many kingdoms. It was mischief, and only mischief, that he did; and though the scale on which he perpetrated mischief was great, his fickleness and vacillation deprived it altogether of the dignity of greatness. His crimes against the peace and welfare of mankind did not arise from any peculiar depravity; he was, on the contrary, naturally of a noble and generous spirit, though in process of time, through the reaction of his conduct upon his heart, these good qualities almost entirely disappeared. Still, he seems never really to have wished mankind ill. He perpetrated his crimes against them thoughtlessly, merely for the purpose of showing what great things he could do.

THE END

ABOUT JACOB ABBOTT

Jacob Abbott was born in Hallowell, Maine in 1803, the son of a minister and farmer. Even as a young boy, he showed academic promise and an interest in spiritual matters. After attending the Hallowell Academy, he was admitted to Bowdoin College at the age of 14.

At Bowdoin, Abbott studied classics and mathematics. He graduated second in his class in 1820 at the young age of 16. He was known as a serious and studious young man who strove for excellence.

After college, Abbott went on to study at Andover Theological Seminary with the intention of becoming a Congregationalist minister. However, his rigorous study habits and frail health caused him to abandon this pursuit after just two years.

Abbott was plagued by gastrointestinal issues and migraines throughout his life, likely exacerbated by the demanding academic environment. His poor health finally forced him to leave his ministerial studies and turn to the less stressful pursuits of writing and tutoring.

First, Abbott took a job as a professor of mathematics and natural philosophy at Amherst College in 1824. The following year, he married Harriet Vaughan and moved to Boston where he opened a school for young ladies. It was during this time that he began writing simple textbooks for teaching science, history and Christian values.

So while Abbott had aspired to be a minister, chronic health issues led him to find an alternate calling educating children through clear and engaging writing. This pivot would launch his successful career as one of the most famous children's authors of the 19th century.

In 1825, Abbott married Harriet Vaughan and soon after started his own school for young ladies in Boston. During this time, he began writing educational books in a popular, simple style. His early works included the Mount Vernon Reader and The Young Christian.

Abbott gained fame with the Rollo series, first published in 1835. These stories followed a young boy named Rollo learning morals and virtues through his everyday adventures. The series was hugely popular and established Abbott's reputation as a gifted children's writer.

Other notable books by Abbott include the Franconia Stories (1853-1873), a 10-volume series about a brother and sister's adventures in the country, and the Marco Paul series (1853-1873), which followed a boy's travels around America learning about each state.

In all, Jacob Abbott wrote over 200 books, primarily for young readers. His works were praised for their ability to educate and impart moral lessons in an engaging, story-driven way. Though largely forgotten today, he was one of the most prolific and beloved children's authors of his era.

Abbott continued writing up until his death on October 31, 1879 in Farmington, Maine. His legacy lives on through his contributions to 19th century children's literature.

BIOGRAPHIES ABBOTT WROTE

A number of the books Abbott wrote were biographies of famous people. Famous characters covered in these books included:

Alexander the Great: This book provides a sweeping look at the life and achievements of Alexander III of Macedon, better known as Alexander the Great. It follows his early education by Aristotle, ascension to the throne after his father Philip II's assassination, and extensive military campaigns across Asia and northeast Africa. Abbott recounts Alexander's major battles against the Persians and annexation of their empire. The book also examines Alexander's tactics, military innovations, and creation of a Hellenistic empire stretching from Greece to India before his death at 32.

Alfred the Great: This biography focuses on Alfred's defense of the Kingdom of Wessex against Viking raids in 9th century England. It discusses how Alfred drove back the Great Heathen Army and then negotiated terms with the Vikings, designating parts of England for their settlement. Abbott also highlights Alfred's efforts to revive learning and education in England, as well as his codification of laws and strengthening of the Anglo-Saxon navy. The book frames Alfred as a scholarly, strategic and devout ruler whose achievements laid the foundation for a unified England.

King Charles I: This book looks at the reign of Charles I leading up to and during the English Civil War. It focuses on the religious and political conflicts between Charles I and Parliament, caused largely by

Charles' belief in divine right of kings and many unpopular, authoritarian policies. Abbott also examines Charles' refusal to compromise, leading to the war against Parliament's New Model Army and his eventual execution for treason in 1649 under Oliver Cromwell.

King Charles II: This biography deals with the restoration of the English monarchy under Charles II after the death of Oliver Cromwell. It follows Charles II's return from exile and re-establishment of royal power. However, Abbott also notes Charles' own conflicts with Parliament and religious controversies during his reign. The book discusses Charles' hedonistic lifestyle and many mistresses, but also his support for science, exploration and trade that helped expand the British Empire.

Cleopatra: This book examines Cleopatra VII's life and rule over ancient Egypt. Abbott chronicles Cleopatra's relationships and political alliances with Julius Caesar and Mark Antony, as she sought to maintain Egypt's independence from Rome. The biography highlights Cleopatra's intelligence, education and strategic skills in dealing with Rome. But it ultimately focuses on Cleopatra's downfall and suicide after Mark Antony's defeat by Octavian, leading to Egypt becoming a Roman province.

Cyrus the Great: This biography covers Cyrus II of Persia, founder of the Achaemenid Empire. Abbott traces Cyrus's rise from Persian prince, to revolt against the Medes, to conqueror of the Lydian and Babylonian empires. The book also examines Cyrus's leadership qualities and tolerant policies toward conquered peoples. It portrays Cyrus as a wise, inspirational leader who created the model of a centralized Persian state.

Darius: This book looks at the reign of Darius I, examining his consolidation of the Persian Empire through administrative reforms, development of infrastructure, and expansion of territory. Abbott discusses

Darius's division of the empire into provinces and implementation of a uniform tax system and coinage. The biography also covers his invasion of Greece which was thwarted at the famous Battle of Marathon. Overall, it presents Darius as an capable, pragmatic ruler under whom the Persian Empire reached its zenith.

Queen Elizabeth: This biography celebrates the long and prosperous reign of Queen Elizabeth I of England. Abbott focuses on Elizabeth's shrewd leadership, religious compromise, and patronage of the arts and literature that fostered English Renaissance culture. The book also highlights Elizabeth's naval defeat of the Spanish Armada which secured England's independence from Europe. Overall, Abbott portrays Elizabeth as a commanding, canny and popular female ruler who strengthened England as a major world power.

Genghis Khan: This book looks at the incredible rise of Temüjin, better known as Genghis Khan. It follows his hardships as an outcast youth to becoming the fearsome founder of the Mongol Empire. Abbott chronicles Genghis Khan's brilliant military tactics and utterly ruthless conquests that allowed the Mongols to dominate much of Asia and Eastern Europe. Overall it paints him as a complex figure--strategic genius but also brutal tyrant.

Hannibal: This biography focuses on the great Carthaginian general Hannibal Barca. It recounts his famous crossing of the Alps with war elephants and invasion of Italy during the Second Punic War against Rome. Abbott details Hannibal's victories in major battles like Cannae but also his eventual defeat by Scipio and exile. The book celebrates Hannibal's daring military prowess but also concession late in life that Rome could not be conquered.

Josephine: This book examines the life of Josephine Bonaparte from her aristocratic upbringing in Martinique to her marriage to Napoleon Bonaparte. It focuses on Josephine's time as Empress consort of France

| 175 |

and her support for arts and education. But it also discusses Napoleon's eventual divorce from her due to dynastic pressures. Overall the book presents Josephine as an intelligent, compassionate woman who tempered some of Napoleon's ambition.

Julius Caesar: This traces Caesar's life from early military campaigns to dictator and eventual assassination. Abbott covers Caesar's conquest of Gaul, rivalry with Pompey, famously crossing the Rubicon and crowning as dictator. The biography also examines the conspiracy led by Brutus and Cassius to assassinate Caesar in order to save the Roman Republic. In all, the book presents Caesar as an unmatched military mind who irrevocably changed the Roman Empire.

Margaret of Anjou: This biography looks at Margaret of Anjou who became queen consort to England's King Henry VI. It focuses on the political intrigue and machinations Margaret became involved in to support her husband's reign during the War of the Roses. Abbott portrays Margaret as a fiercely devoted, cunning woman who backed the Lancastrians against factions like the Yorkists led by Richard Neville. Though she lost power, the book frames her as a dominant figure during the conflict.

Mary, Queen of Scots: This book examines the life of Mary Stuart who became Queen of Scotland as an infant. It follows her tumultuous reign marked by scandals and plots to overthrow her by Protestants. Her Catholicism also put her at odds with England's Elizabeth I. Abbott recounts Mary's forced abdication, escape to England, and eventual execution ordered by Elizabeth for plotting against her. Overall it presents a tragic figure whose life was marked by political and religious turmoil.

Nero: This biography looks at the notorious Roman emperor Nero. It explores his self-indulgent lifestyle and tyrannical rule marked by possible matricide and the brutal execution of Christians. Abbott also examines legends around Nero like his fiddling during the Great Fire of Rome. The book presents a despotic, unstable man who drastically weakened the Roman Empire.

Peter the Great: This book covers the reforms and policies of Peter the Great that rapidly westernized Russia. Abbott discusses Peter's extensive European travels as a youth and later programs to remake Russia's army, expand its naval fleet, and build a new capital in St. Petersburg. The biography also examines Peter's harsh, authoritarian approach to governing that consolidated his power. Overall it presents him as a pivotal, transformative tsar.

Pyrrhus: This examines the life and military exploits of Pyrrhus, king of Epirus. It focuses on his campaigns against Rome where he won major battles but suffered heavy losses, giving rise to the term "Pyrrhic victory." Abbott recounts Pyrrhus's struggles to build a Greek empire and failed invasion of Sicily against Carthage. Though a skilled commander, Pyrrhus ultimately failed to achieve lasting gains.

Richard I: This biography looks at the reign of Richard I, known as Lionheart. It focuses on Richard's leadership during the Third Crusade to recapture Jerusalem from Saladin. Abbott also details the legendary tales of Richard's bravery and valor in campaigns against France and during his imprisonment. Overall, the book presents Richard I as one of England's great warrior kings.

Richard II: This explores the reign and overthrow of King Richard II. Abbott covers Richard's despotic actions that led the nobles to revolt and install Henry IV, leading to Richard's imprisonment and likely murder. The biography presents a weak king whose tyranny and poor leadership during a peasant's revolt cost him power and his life.

Richard III: This delves into the controversial rule of Richard III. Abbott examines Richard's contested path to the throne and the disappearance of the Princes in the Tower which Richard likely ordered. It also portrays Richard's defeat at the hands of Henry Tudor at the Battle of Bosworth Field that ended the Wars of the Roses. Ultimately Abbott paints Richard III as willing to employ any means to gain and retain the English crown.

Romulus: This recounts the Roman legend of Romulus and Remus, twin brothers raised by a she-wolf who went on to found the city of Rome. Abbott covers the myths of the brothers' quarrel over leadership, with Romulus killing Remus and becoming Rome's first king and architect of its nascent political institutions. Though mythological, Romulus represents ancient Rome's founding origins and rise to power.

William the Conqueror: This biography follows William, Duke of Normandy's conquest of England in 1066 after victory at the Battle of Hastings. Abbott discusses William's reign as king where he consolidated control, introduced feudalism, and fused English and Norman culture. William is presented as a formidable, innovative Norman leader who irrevocably transformed Anglo-Saxon England.

Xerxes: This examines the reign of Xerxes I of Persia, known for his failed invasion of Greece. Abbott focuses on Xerxes's gathering of a massive army to crush Greek resistance, but defeat at Salamis ended his ambitions. The book covers later unrest and palace intrigue that clouded the end of Xerxes's reign. Overall he is portrayed as a rash ruler whose desire for conquest led to disaster for Persia.

www.ingramcontent.com/pod-product-compliance
Lightning Source LLC
Chambersburg PA
CBHW070059080526
44586CB00013B/1119